# MOTOR MANIA

# MOTOR MANIA

## A Hundred Years of Motoring

### RICHARD SUTTON

**PAST TIMES**™
Oxford, England

First published in Great Britain in 1996
by Collins & Brown Limited, London House,
Great Eastern Wharf, Parkgate Road, London  SW11 4NQ

This edition published 1996 for PAST TIMES˙ Oxford, England

British Library Cataloguing-in-Publication Data: A catalogue record for this
book is available from the British Library.

ISBN 1 85585 260 8 (hardback)
ISBN 1 85585 270 5 (paperback)
1 3 5 7 9 8 6 4 2

Edited by Toucan Books Limited

Designed by Bradbury & Williams

Picture research by Robin Gurdon

Senior Editor: Liz Dean

Reproduction by Daylight, Singapore
Printed and bound by Hunter and Foulis, Edinburgh

Every reasonable effort has been made to ensure the accuracy of
information in this book. Although the Author and the Publishers can
accept no responsibility for errors or inaccuracies, the Publishers welcome
reader comment or information, which may be used in future printings.

FRONT COVER: Advertisement for Morris Isis Six, 1930.
Illustrated London News/ The Mary Evans Picture Library

BACK COVER: Advertisement for Humber cars, 1907.
National Motor Museum, Beaulieu

OPPOSITE TITLE PAGE: Vauxhall 30/98, National Motor
Museum, Beaulieu

# CONTENTS

# INTRODUCTION

The British motor industry was effectively founded on 14th January 1896 when the mercurial and notorious entrepreneur Harry Lawson filed the patents for the British Daimler Company. At that time there were approximately 20 cars in Britain. In 1996, as the owners of the Daimler marque, Jaguar Cars, celebrate Daimler's 100th anniversary, there are a million times that number.

Such a staggering and unprecedented rate of industrial expansion, together with the growth of the infrastructures that are reliant on the motor industry, has ensured that the well-being of the British economy relies on the widespread existence of motoring. In 1995 approximately 70 per cent of British households owned at least one car, and the volume is expected to grow to encompass virtually every household over the next decade, despite the fact road-building is likely to increase during that time by no more than around 5 per cent. Furthermore, motoring in Britain causes traffic congestion costing the country 1.2 billion working hours a year at an annual cost of £520 per household, according to the CBI. Add to these worrying statistics the thousands of tons of lead and carbon monoxide that cars emit into Britain's atmosphere every year, to say nothing of the continued demise of fossil fuel stocks, and it would be only natural to assume that motoring was perceived by the general public as unfashionable, if not intolerable.

*You are what you drive: an obvious aesthete settles himself in a unique 1922 Peugeot Quadrilette. Although the Peugeot was a volume-produced car, this example has a built-to-order, one-off body and interior, possibly executed by an independent Parisian coachbuilder.*

Nothing, in fact, could be further from the truth. This motoring monster, which holds our economy together while threatening to blow our environment apart, continues to appeal on a growing and extraordinary scale. At least three major national weekend newspapers sport huge sections dedicated exclusively to motoring; large swathes of newsagents' shelves are devoted to motoring magazines; motoring television programmes are consistently among the most widely watched; and Formula One motor racing is the Western world's most popular sport, between 600 and 800 million watching each race on television. Despite the environmental and social implications – to say nothing of the daily aggravations and considerable cost of personal motoring in the 1990s – motor mania is rife.

But motoring today is not the mania that it was. Before the First World War, just to see a car was the great highlight of the day for many a keen schoolboy. Even until the Second World War, to drive or ride in a car was a

relatively unusual experience for most people, and actually to own one was a middle or upper-class privilege indeed. Although the idea of 'motoring for the masses' was put into action by the larger manufacturers during the thirties, the Second World War and the austerity it left in its wake ensured that motoring for average people was still unusual until the sixties. And with the expansion of the market and the mass-production methods needed to build enough cars, traffic levels and legislation strangled the motoring dream. As a result, driving lost its appeal and cars lost their character. True freedom of the road had vanished by the time the novelty of post-austerity Britain was over in the early sixties.

Of course, it's not all doom and gloom. Advances made in car design and production methods, particularly during the seventies and early eighties, have created cars that are not only as cheap as they have ever been in relation to average incomes, but also far superior as reliable, comfortable, usable products. As I write, in 1995, a ten-year-old car in well-maintained condition is more or less as capable as its modern equivalent, but in 1985 a ten-year-old car would have been a far more risky proposition. Over the last 20 years, design and construction techniques have leapt forward; corrosion prevention and more reliable component designs have revolutionised the

*A rare picture of the film star Rudolf Valentino posing by his very impressive 1925 Voisin 4-litre CS. Valentino was a great lover of cars and this French Voisin was among the world's most expensive, exclusive and exceptional automobiles.*

*An excellent example of pre-Second World War customising. This motorist clearly has ideas above his station, having added polished aluminium 'ace discs' to his lowly Austin. Such items were usually confined to far more expensive cars, and their fitting to an Austin says plenty about the driver's aspirations.*

motor car, and the end of international labour strikes and disruptive mergers has placed the international motor industry on a much sounder footing. All this holds true despite the need for enormous investment to maintain national prowess in car design and production in the midst of ever more stringent environmental and safety legislation. In short, quite apart from the incalculable industrial obstacles, the motorist has never had as much choice, or such able cars, for as little money as he or she has today.

However, as the 300,000 or so people who buy classic car magazines every month in Great Britain will vouch, motoring has become perceived as an essential need rather than a joyful prospect. Haven't cars become so alike and so bland that it is now impossible to relate to them as anything but utilitarian machines? They used to arouse deep nostalgic emotions; they used to be members of the family, trusty servants, characters to be washed and waxed, serviced and nurtured. After all, such unconditional love would ensure the car's faithful service. Cars were given names, and tears would be shed when one was sold, particularly by children who related to the family car as their magic carpet on which they would travel to wondrous places, all secure in the knowledge that it would bring them home in time for bed.

The Sunday drive is an almost quaint prospect today, but until the end of the fifties it was commonplace. Today, most people would sooner book a package holiday by plane than load up the car with butterfly nets, thermos flasks, pup tent and gas stove for a motoring trip among the hedgerows and byways of Old England.

The enthusiasm for motoring in the fifties was hardly surprising. With the war and substandard 'pool' petrol finally a thing of the past (the latter only disappearing in 1953), with roads repaired, a high proportion of the adult population in work, and many a new model of car on the market, the freedom that motoring represented was a powerful tonic. However, although the fifties' up-beat feeling was epitomised by such splendid new British sports cars as the Jaguar XK120 (1949), Triumph TR2 (1952), Austin-Healey 100 (1952) and the MG A (1955), for the most part Britain's automobile offerings were pretty dull. Austin A40s were probably the best of the baby car bunch, while the commodious five-star Fords – Consul, Zephyr and Zodiac – were capable mid-priced family saloons that at least cut a fashionable, if rather American, dash. Advanced continental products were now set to flood into Britain, especially after the 1956 Suez Crisis brought back petrol rationing for a brief but ultimately salutary period. 'Suez' was enough to demonstrate to manufacturers and customers alike that petrol was not a resource that could be squandered, even outside wartime, and fuel economy became an important consideration in the design of cars. The continentals produced an excellent selection of economy cars, and until the revolutionary Mini appeared in 1959, and to a lesser extent the excellent Triumph Herald in the same year, the British had little that was comparably 'state-of-the-art'.

*An interesting period comparison between the popular British Ford Consul (top) and the equivalent French family car, the Peugeot 403 (bottom). The Ford had lots of American influence in its styling, reflecting the nationality of its parent company, while the Peugeot was more elegant and European.*

Fortunately, a certain degree of prejudice against foreign cars still lingered – their sales and service back-ups and marque reputations were not yet established in Britain, and import costs were relatively high – otherwise the dreary British marque line-ups would have surely been swamped by the technically advanced wares from Alfa Romeo (the dynamic Giulietta range), Fiat (the charming 500 Topolino), Citroën (the sensationally advanced DS and remarkable 2CV), Peugeot (the elegant Pininfarina 403s) and Renault (the chic Dauphines and ever-so capable 4CVs), to say nothing of the legendary Volkswagen Beetle.

The import tide was further delayed by Britain's late entry into the Common Market, tariffs rendering foreign cars expensive in relation to their domestic rivals. But the coming of the foreign car was as inevitable as foreign investment in Britain's car industry. The French Citroën company and Italian Fiat concern had been building cars in Britain since long before the Second World War; the American General Motors organisation bought the prized British Vauxhall

## RED DANIELLS REMEMBERS – YOU ARE WHAT YOU DRIVE

*'There was a certain gentleman I recall who owned an Armstrong-Siddeley. He used to bring it to our garage for servicing. That car suited him down to the ground. He was a little fat man with a winged collar. He was very proper and respectable, never smiled and his wife was never allowed to speak. I think I heard her complete half a sentence once, that was about it. Anyway, one day this man said he'd like to buy this wrecked Bentley we had. We'd all been wondering what to do with it and were delighted that he wanted us to restore it for him. So we rebuilt it – gave it the full treatment, copper exhaust, that sort of thing, and it was a beautiful car. When he took delivery he had great difficulty in driving it away and one of us had to go with him to make sure he got it home to Highgate. Anyway, I didn't see him for another six months and then, one Sunday going past a pub in Highgate, I saw the old Bentley parked outside. So I stopped and went inside and there was the owner in the open-necked shirt and the Fairisle sweater, the coloured corduroy trousers and two-tone shoes, standing there at the bar laying down the law about Vintage cars being so much better than the modern rubbish out there in the car park. It was our chap, and he'd changed completely to suit the car. And might I say that he took me round the block in the Bentley and he drove it very well. Yes, he was arrogant and patronising, but that's what you expect from the driver of a motor car like that.'*

company in 1925, while its compatriot, the Ford Motor Company, set up its huge Dagenham plant in 1932. Faced with a motley selection of small manufacturing companies, Britain's export-led motor industry had to pool its resources to survive. The result was the British Motor Corporation, and its cars, like so many offerings from big, rationalised foreign manufacturers, rapidly evolved into many models which relied upon packaging and marketing, rather than significant design factors, to tell them apart.

Packaging took on added significance when the Japanese invaded the European car markets during the 1960s, an export drive of such magnitude that the Japanese motor industry grew from being the sixth largest in the world in 1961 to the second largest in just ten years. Only the enormous size of America's industry could surpass Japan's soaring output – a monumental achievement from a country economically devastated after the Second World War and possessing insignificant automotive raw materials. The Japanese car relied upon low price and a careful eye on economy and packaging to carve its market niche in Britain. Never before had regular styling changes and high equipment levels been considered so important.

With performance, accommodation and economy specifications getting ever closer among the various rival marques and manufacturers, image and style became a new priority in the motor business, and have

*Below: 'I've got a 3-litre Rover at the moment – about a mile outside Salford'.*

remained so ever since. Today 'you are what you drive' as never before, and manufacturers see personal identity as a more and more important factor in selling cars. A letter in *Autocar* responding to the launch of *Goldeneye*, the first new 'James Bond' film for six years, commented that James Bond had turned from secret agent to estate agent now that the new Bond car was a BMW convertible. But typecasting the characters and professions of motorists according to what car they drive is nothing new. Brand loyalty and marque image are as old as the industry, even if they weren't considered such a powerful marketing tool.

In the earliest days of the motor business foreign cars were entirely acceptable and, until the coming of the Rolls-Royce Ghost in 1907, they were probably the best. After the First World War, by which time the late-developing British motor industry was among the world leaders, patriotism became very important. Although American imports sold well at the time, if only because they were more readily available during the austerity years, you had to be seriously cosmopolitan or have authentic celebrity status to run an Hispano-Suiza or a Bugatti, a Lancia or an Alfa Romeo, at all credibly.

Well-heeled young men before the Second World War would probably be seen driving MGs or Rileys, while Austins and Morrises were typically confined to those who motored out of necessity rather than indulgence. Just as it is today, the motorist's aspiration to gain more status on the road was embarrassingly common: the MG owner

*Perhaps the most significant automobile of the motoring century: the new-for-1959 BMC Mini. It probably incorporated more revolutionary design features than any car before or since and remains in popular production to this day.*

dreamt of possessing a Triumph Dolomite or fantasised about an Aston Martin, just as the Austin or Morris owner longed for the upper-crust respectability of a Wolseley or Rover.

Until the 1950s, Royalty nearly always drove Daimlers, while until the 1960s civil servants, bank managers and accountants drove either Humbers or Armstrong-Siddeleys. Rolls-Royces were always considered to be rather bourgeois, just as they are arguably today, while Bentleys were altogether more dashing. Trojans were for vicars, Vauxhalls were for doctors, SSs and Jaguars were for cads and traders, while Singers were owned by the successful boy next door of whom mother would approve.

The advent of 'badge engineering', largely initiated by manufacturing groups after the Second World War, made a mockery of marque-buyer associations. From this time onwards, Rolls-Royces and Bentleys, for example, would be essentially the same cars, only the radiator grilles and various fixtures and fittings telling them apart. Yet the self-styled sportsman still bought the Bentley, while the *nouveau riche* remained loyal to the

*Women have been ruthlessly used by the motor industry to sell 'sexy' cars, as both Porsche (top) and Reliant laughably demonstrate.*

Rolls-Royce. The image scenario with the more recent Jaguar/Daimler badge is similar: two very different types of customer being lured to buy essentially identical cars. In fact, the image of the Jaguar car is a poignant example of how fortunes are fixed by such superficialities. Jaguar cars (much more so than their near-identical Daimler stable-mates) have traditionally been perceived as being driven by those with 'more flash than cash', and it is only relatively recently that Jaguar has lost the crippling caddish image. The reputation was born out of the fact that Jaguar cars, right from their inception as SS cars in 1931, offered looks and performance not unlike their contemporary Rolls-Royces and Bentleys but always at a fraction of their price. But that was in the days when the unrestricted car stylist was largely responsible for the car's image, with little help from marketing departments and advertising agencies.

Today, car design and image-making are much more challenging tasks. Design for mass-produced cars is now restricted by so many criteria that the sweep of the stylist's pen is dictated more by component rationalisation and safety features than by anything more spiritual. While the designer's challenge has always been to work around the obstacles that exist to make a motor car perform as it is required to do, the sharing of common bodyshells between manufacturers, to say nothing of engines and drive-trains, severely restricts the designer's flair. And as manufacturers in different countries, even continents, endeavour to rationalise car design further so that similar cars will sell in all markets, so more and more responsibility is left with the packagers, marketing specialists and advertisers. They must ensure that a new model has an image to sell, quite apart from the new car's inevitable technological advances.

With so many restrictions on and requirements for today's car designers, and with myriad problems facing the motorist, environmentalist and automotive industrialist alike, it is little wonder that much of the romance has been lost from motoring, the car becoming little more than a mundane, sometimes despised workhorse.

Featuring a wealth of period motoring ephemera, and a rich variety of interviews with dozens of enthusiasts, *Motor Mania* is all about motoring nostalgia. This book is about the birth of motoring: those who invented and manufactured cars, the salesmen and the garagists, the supporting organisations and trades – the people who made motoring possible in the face of continuous opposition and those who brought the freedom of the road to the masses. But above all, *Motor Mania* is about those who motored from the pioneering days to the end of the post-Second World War austerity years. It's a whimsical collection of anecdotes, stories, facts and figures that chart the progress of a century-old industry which has become a vital constituent of the world's economic axis.

*Motor mania has reshaped Britain's landscape, and new road-building appears to be an unavoidable evil perpetuated to cope with the ever-rising number of vehicles on the move. This is the ugly construction of part of the M1 in 1965.*

# Chapter 1

## THE PIONEERS

*I* like motoring because I have suffered for its sake... My agonies, shames, delays, rages, chills, parboilings, road-walkings, water-drawings, burns and starvations – at which you laughed – all went to make your car today safe and comfortable... Any fool can invent anything, as any fool can wait to buy the invention when it is thoroughly perfected, but the men to reverence, to admire, to write odes and erect statues to, are those Prometheuses and Ixions (maniacs, you used to call us) who chase the inchoate idea to fixity up and down the King's Highway with their red right shoulders to the wheel... I love because I have suffered... in the cause of Humanity. RUDYARD KIPLING, 1904.

Assuming that you weren't alive at the time, it is probably too fantastic to imagine a world without automobiles. Yet a century ago, the motor car had arguably existed for no more than 11 years and had yet to be manufactured at all in Great Britain. To a society that relied almost totally upon the horse for its domestic mobility, the concept that a human-fangled device could do a better job than the Lord's own Dobbin was completely daft. I make no assumptions about this: read any thorough account of the life and times of the early automobile inventors and the alarming prejudice with which their creations were received is rife. For the first 20 years of its existence motoring suffered the wrath of a damning public.

*Above: No, it's not a gravy boat. It's Jean Hautsch's whimsical mechanical vehicle which was enough to cut a dash in the most fashionable high street in 1649.*

*Pages 14-15: The nonchalant Hon Evelyn Ellis (left) poses on his Panhard at Britain's first automotive gathering, staged at Tunbridge Wells in October 1895. Five vehicles were exhibited; 5000 spectators attended.*

We should have no delusions of charm about the horse-drawn ages. While today's nostalgia might portray an era of immaculate carriages and their handsome teams, bustling street scenes of dashing horsemen and gaily-attired travellers, the truth was often far from that. Where horse-drawn traffic occurred with any kind of regularity the roads were rutted, filthy and impregnated with excrement, much of which would accumulate before being washed into the earth and wood-block roads by urine and rainwater. As a result, busy thoroughfares usually stank and were breeding grounds for all kinds of disease. And the dramatic dust clouds produced by speeding traffic on a dry day were not the rooster-tails of romantic travel, but clouds of dried faeces and dirt, which would settle on everything from hair-dos to washing hung out to dry.

While it is true that Dobbin was a companion of sorts and had a good deal more character than even the most unreliable machine, he came with all manner of complications. He consumed a costly bulk of hay and oats; he required frequent rest (and continued to absorb food when doing so); he didn't move very quickly or for very long, so that teams of Dobbins were required for long trips; he demanded full-time staff to look after him and clean up wherever he had been. Not unreasonably, Dobbin sometimes

*Left: From* Punch *in 1900: 'Mr Jenkins drove his new motor car down to Epsom, but to be sure of arriving there, he thought it wise to bring his horses as well.'*

*Below: Numerous attempts were made to deal with the road dust problem. Here a binding compound called 'Westrumite' is sprayed from a water cart at Crystal Palace in 1903.*

*Right: In 1833 a Dr Church conceived this wondrous 50-seater, three-wheeled steam coach. Although beautifully decorated, such heavy-weight fantasies were wholly impractical, unlike the utilitarian steam tractor (below) which successfully established the credibility of steam vehicles against the traditional horse.*

didn't feel very well – which could cost his master dearly until Dob' got his pace back – and if ever he got seriously hurt, he might find himself woefully betrayed, the knacker's yard being his likely destiny. Add such bothersome factors to the filthy roads which Dobbins (and even Muffins) of all shapes and sizes perpetuated, and it is not hard to see why the invention of the automobile might have been considered a rather good thing.

But that wasn't the case at all.

In reality, the great automotive pioneers were continually struggling against the odds to develop their visions. The pioneers' story is one of relentless battles: battles against engineering and environmental obstacles; battles against patenting regulations; battles against the police and those in the legislature; battles against the general public – particularly those in the horse business; and battles against each other.

## THE FIRST INVENTORS

Deciding who can claim to have invented the automobile is an awkward issue, because it rather depends on what one considers an automobile to be. According to the *Concise Oxford Dictionary* an automobile is 'a motor car', and a motor car is... 'a car with a motor engine', a motor being, not surprisingly, 'what imparts motion'. Such ponderous definitions place the birth of the automobile anywhere between the years 1672 and 1769, depending on what you choose to believe. However, if we regard the car as a vehicle powered specifically by an internal-combustion engine, the birthdate can be more accurately placed in the 19th century, anywhere between the years 1826 and 1875. Add another vital criterion, namely the use of a four-stroke power cycle to the internal-combustion engine (a system which is the corner-stone of the popular motor car engine to this day), and the birthdate is probably 1875.

While those faithful to their own nationalities and creeds will doubtless support their man as the inventor of the automobile, one thing is certain: the fathers of the *commercial* automobile were Karl Benz and Gottlieb Daimler. It was Karl Benz who indisputedly created and manufactured the first successful automobile to be produced in quantity in 1885, while Gottlieb Daimler, whose first car appeared a year later than Benz's, created and developed the most mechanically advanced automobile of its generation. In the light of Benz's and Daimler's achievements, the feat of creating a vehicle that moved under its own power – admirable though that had been considered in the

### FATHER VERBIEST, CAPTAIN CUGNOT AND THE FIRST HORSELESS CARRIAGE

Although the earliest horseless carriage inventions relied on all manner of propulsion methods, including wind, levers and springs, it was steam power that gave the horseless carriage some serious oomph. Remarkably, the first steam carriage was successfully built and demonstrated either in 1672 by the Jesuit priest Father Verbiest, at the commission of the then Chinese Emperor, or in 1769 by the French Artillery Captain Nicholas-Joseph Cugnot. Cugnot's 12-minute, 6mph demonstration of his massive 5-ton, steam-powered gun-carrier is well known and documented. Furthermore, his carriage exists for all to see at the Conservatoire des Arts et Métiers in Paris, which helps his claim to fame enormously. Father Verbiest's achievements are less easy to verify. His car apparently ran successfully and 'with a great velocity as long as the steam lasted', according to Abbé Hue, who documents the vehicle's achievements and specifications in the *Astronomia Europaea*. Apparently Verbiest's car existed until comparatively recently at the Emperor's Winter Palace but, until it is found, Cugnot's monster motor continues to stake its innovative claim.

*Above: Every coachman's nightmare: what is probably a road-hogging Hill Steam Coach demonstrating its bulk and lack of agility. After 1830 such devices became the established transport between Birmingham and London for 15 passengers at a time, reaching speeds of just over 12mph.*

*Below: Captain Cugnot's steam tractor which was arguably the first to run, in 1769.*

past – counted for little if the vehicles could not be made to work consistently and could not be replicated in marketable quantities. Benz and Daimler excelled because they were the first people to perfect their designs and see them through to commercial reality. Quite simply, Benz and Daimler persisted where others gave up.

Yes, Benz and Daimler were Germans, a fact which does not impress the Belgians, British, French and Austrians, all of whom have legitimate claims for supporting their particular men as the first. But this nationalistic squabble opens up a whole new tin of nuts 'n' bolts as to what is, and what is not, an automobile. The key issue is that the automobile *evolved* into being and was not created by one man alone. Benz's and Daimler's historic achievements, however, heralded a new era – the start of the motor industry.

## It began with steam

The process that led to the invention and marketing of the automobile had its roots in the history of the steam-powered horseless carriage. Steam power was at the hub of the Industrial Revolution and found its indispensable value in the railway business where the heavy mechanics, boilers and fuels of steam power could be effectively housed on the chassis of railway locomotives. Although the French physicist Denis Papin invented the steam engine in 1690, it wasn't until 1830 that Stephenson's Rocket locomotive offered a practical application of the technology to rail transport. It was all the more remarkable that as early as 1801 Britain's Richard Trevithick devised the first steam carriage.

The device was reported to have carried seven or eight passengers up Camborne Beacon in Cornwall on Christmas Eve. Unfortunately, though, Trevithick's carriage was destroyed by fire soon afterwards and what might have been a successful foray into steam-car design was curtailed prematurely. Yet the premise had been set, and over the next one hundred years steam became the answer to horseless transport.

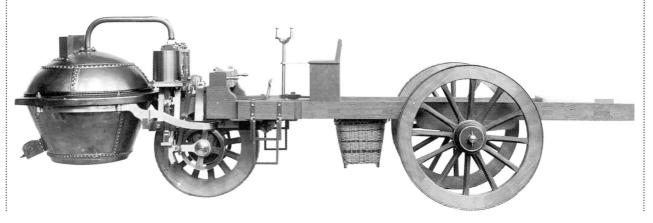

By the beginning of the second quarter of the 19th century, steam-powered coaches were being demonstrated as alternatives to railway travel, offering a more flexible and personal service. Goldsworthy Gurney demonstrated his New Steam Coach at 5mph in London's Regent's Park in 1827, and from 1830 steam-coach operators such as Walter Hancock and Frank Hill began to establish regular long-distance services. Although steam coaches were still a very new invention, there was much public prejudice against them. They were heavy, slow and uncomfortable, and with the relentless expansion of the steam railway network the steam-coach business soon faltered.

The steam coach does, however, play its part in the story of the car. First, the coaches incorporated a number of mechanical innovations which found their way into early automobiles, and some of these – notably independent suspension, differential gears and driveshaft universal joints – are still indispensable in modern cars. Secondly, the coaches demonstrated to some that steam power was not the solution to the transport problem. The copious quantities of coal and water that they demanded, the weight and size of the machinery, and the filthy smoke they produced made the design of small, light steam cars extremely impractical, if not, at that time, inconceivable.

Steam coaches and cars were very much more popular in Italy and France than they ever were in Britain, and the French made great progress in steam-car design. As early as 1878, Amédée Bollée's La Mancelle featured his patented geometrically-correct steering system as well as the now long-established front-engine/rear-wheel-drive layout. La Mancelle even had differential gears and a prop-shaft, and it looked far more like an automobile than either Daimler's or Benz's early efforts. La Mancelle was good for nearly 22mph, and its successor, La Rapide, did more than 37mph in 1881. But the advent of the internal-combustion engine rendered even the 'hot' steam car dated. Bollée and his competitor de Dion embraced the internal-combustion revolution while the great French steam pioneer Serpollet continued to develop his steam ideals until his death in 1907 (see page 26).

(see page 26)

## THE UNSUNG SAMUEL BROWN AND, ARGUABLY, THE FIRST AUTOMOBILE WITH AN INTERNAL-COMBUSTION ENGINE

As early as the mid-1820s an unsung Englishman named Samuel Brown had appreciated the limitations of steam power and designed a slow-burning internal-combustion engine which he demonstrated in his own car on 27th May 1826. Apparently he drove up Shooters Hill in London without a problem. Brown's achievement, although little documented, was monumental, because he not only succeeded in designing the first internal-combustion engine (although one using a slow-burning fuel principle, rather than an explosion of gas), but also demonstrated it in what was perhaps the world's first automobile, too. But Brown's engine was not considered practical; steam power was still in its infancy and showing lots of potential. His invention was shelved, and with little known of it or his engineering principles or his car, his fame looks certain to be unrealised.

## THE INTERNAL-COMBUSTION REVOLUTION

During the middle years of the 19th century, inventors and engineers such as Eugenio Barsanti and Felice Matteuci in Italy, and Etienne Lenoir in Belgium, started to focus on gas-powered engines of the internal-combustion type. Although Samuel Brown in England had made early forays into gas-powered engines (and even built a car powered by one) as early as the 1820s, the major developments were achieved by Barsanti and

Matteuci, and Lenoir. Lenoir built himself a car using one of his engines in 1862, which he allegedly used for his daily commute through Paris's Bois de Vincennes to his home. The following year he made a 6-mile trip from Paris to Joinville-le-Pont and back in three hours but, apart from being frantically slow, his machine suffered considerable water consumption and other breakdowns *en route*. Lenoir then abandoned his automobile ambitions and sold all his patents. He sold his car, incidentally, to Tsar Alexander II Nicolaevitch of Russia (unfortunately, it was destroyed during the Franco-Prussian War).

So Lenoir – like Brown and Barsanti and Matteuci before him (see left, below) – failed to see his invention perfected, but before he gave up he at least inspired two other pioneers, both of whom were to contribute in a major way to the invention of the automobile. One was the aforementioned German, Gottlieb Daimler, who had visited Lenoir in 1860; the other was another German named Nicholas August Otto, a key early engine designer and industrialist who went on to employ Daimler and his assistant Wilhelm Maybach in or around 1866 at his company, Gasmotoren-Fabrik Deutz. In doing this, Otto was sowing the seeds of one of the greatest partnerships in the history of the automobile: that of Daimler and Maybach.

While all this earnest engine development was taking place in north-western Europe, a brilliant Austrian engineer called Siegfried Markus, whose talents ranged from the design and manufacture of dentistry materials to building engines, was busy creating what was the first automobile of any useful worth. Most significantly, it was powered by a four-stroke internal-combustion engine. It was a suitably primitive affair and in its initial form required the driven wheels to be lifted off the ground for the engine to be fired, the wheels then being lowered as the passengers jumped on for their momentous ride. After a premature attempt in 1865, Markus improved his design substantially before demonstrating it to good effect at 4mph over 17 miles in 1875. After that journey, Markus could be seen on various occasions travelling on his automobile, until the local population complained to the police about the noise and general disturbance he caused, and the police put a stop to it. As Markus was no longer allowed to drive his car, there was no way in which he could develop it, and so he abandoned his automobile project after just four examples had been built.

With Lenoir sold up, and Markus forced to stop his experiments, the focus for the conception of the commercially viable automobile lay in Germany. By

---

### AN ITALIAN PRIEST, HIS ENGINEER PARTNER, THEIR BELGIAN RIVAL AND, OFFICIALLY, THE FIRST INTERNAL-COMBUSTION ENGINE

In 1853 the Italians Eugenio Barsanti and Felice Matteuci patented the world's first gas engine, which was successfully demonstrated in 1856. Barsanti (a priest and conceptualiser) and Matteuci (the engineer) designed and built other engines in 1857 and 1858 before exhibiting their most refined version at the National Exhibition in Florence in 1861. Significantly, however, two years earlier the Belgian Jean Joseph Etienne Lenoir had formed the Société des Moteurs, having demonstrated his two-cycle gas engine. Although a better design than the Italians', Lenoir's creation was hardly efficient, producing just 2hp from 18 litres. But such a state-of-the-art device sold well, and 500 units found customers over the next five years. Although Barsanti and Matteuci applied through the British consul in Livorno in 1861 for a patent for 'obtaining motive power by the explosion of gases', Lenoir secured his patent in January 1860 for 'an engine dilated by the combustion of gas'. In any case, the Italians split up (Matteuci retired, Barsanti died of typhoid) and Lenoir secured their patent. Furthermore, Lenoir devised a system whereby his engine would run without the need for a fixed supply of gas. This meant that his engine could be used in a personal carriage, and so it was, in 1862.

1875 Daimler and Maybach had created a highly successful company for Otto and his financial partner Langen, producing well over 600 free-piston engines a year. Furthermore, Daimler and Maybach had also developed Otto's long-abandoned four-stroke engine theories and produced a successful engine. However, having done this, Otto attempted to monopolise the market with patents for the design. These were overruled in 1886 following a long legal battle, after it was found that a French engineer, Alphonse Beau de Rochas, had detailed the four-stroke principle in papers compiled as early as 1862. Ironically, Otto had abandoned the principle a year before de Rochas' writings. This was a fortunate mishap for the industry, because without Otto's patent monopoly the rest of the industry could race to develop the excellent four-stroke engine and its applications. Daimler and Maybach saw their chance. They left Otto and set to work in the garden shed of Daimler's home in Cannstatt. The year was 1881.

## BENZ'S EARLY JOURNEYS

While Daimler and Maybach concentrated their efforts on engine design, Karl Benz was concerning himself with designing a self-propelled velocipede. The velocipede was a light three-wheeler on which a man could self-propel himself at anything up to 12mph. In 1883 Benz, with the help of

*Karl Benz (right) and Josef Brecht atop a Benz Patent Motorwagen in 1887. The Benz three-wheeler was the world's first successful commercially manufactured automobile.*

financial backers, set about designing what amounted to his automobile. His 985cc four-stroke engine (using Otto's principles) produced 0.75hp and was fuelled by benzine, an early version of petrol which could be bought through chemists' shops.

Using his home-made spark plug and carburettor, Benz's rear-engined three-wheeler showed early promise. His initial demonstrations were terminated prematurely, however, due to mechanical problems, despite a speed of 8mph being achieved on only the car's second run. Consequently, the engine was enlarged and the wheels and gearing improved before more extended tests were undertaken in Mannheim under cover of darkness. Like Markus before him, Benz was constantly wary of the public's complaints and the possibility that the police would ban his invention altogether. Benz had targeted a circling route around Mannheim. The second circle was wide, its path moving further away from the factory as the reliability of the car improved. It was the summer of 1886 when, after many attempts, the full route was successfully completed and a triumphant Benz and his passenger returned the car, for the first time, to the factory in the same condition in which it had left. In the words of the author Phil Drackett: 'From the time of that journey, it can truthfully be said, the automobile age had dawned.'

Unfortunately, the birth of the automobile age brought with it innumerable infancy problems. Most immediate among these for Benz was the police in a country with a 4mph speed limit, and, secondly, the lack of customers for his device. The former, at least in his immediate locality, seemed easier to deal with than the latter. By offering to take the local chief of police for a ride in his new car, Benz was quickly able to demonstrate not only the marvellous potential of the automobile but also how restricting the speed limit was. Unbeknown to the police officer, Benz arranged for a milk wagon to hold up their journey, albeit at the usual horses' pace, and the agitated police chief soon agreed that the new invention could and should be allowed to travel faster.

But Benz's local successes with the police were insignificant to the buying public; in the early years of the automobile the speed limit constricted development and sales more seriously than any other factor. This was just one reason why, despite the success of his invention, Benz found it impossible to sell his cars. Following Benz's successful demonstration of the car at the Paris Exhibition in 1887, and another award-winning display of his improved two-speed, 2hp version at the Power Machinery Exhibition in Munich in 1888, some sales seemed only logical, but they just didn't happen.

KARL BENZ DRIVES HIS AUTOMOBILE FOR THE FIRST TIME AND SECURES GERMAN PATENT 37/435 ON 29TH JANUARY 1886

Whatever the arguments regarding who invented the automobile, Karl Benz was indisputably the first to make his invention a commercial reality, and 29th January 1886 may be considered the birthday of the world motor industry. Although Benz had a serious national rival in Gottlieb Daimler, Daimler was preoccupied with engine development rather than automobile design. Daimler, however, was later to take the lead from Benz, and it was his patents sold internationally, particularly via Sarazin to Panhard Levassor in France, that spurred on the world business. Unfortunately, Benz remained unbending in his methods, and his innovations soon became outdated as Daimler and his partner Maybach, among others, improved on the early designs. Benz production peaked in 1899 when his 2000th car was delivered. After that time the company declined and then struggled before eventually being bought by Daimler in 1926. Daimler-Benz remains one of the world's most successful motor manufacturers to this day, selling its cars under the name 'Mercedes-Benz'.

Karl Benz's wife, Bertha, so frustrated at the lack of public belief in her husband's invention, even went so far as to steal Karl's car one night and drive it, with her two sons on board, 62 miles to Pforzheim. This epic journey – the like of which had never been attempted before – firmly established Bertha as one of the heroic pioneers of the automobile. Bertha and her sons completed the trip with plenty of uphill pushing but without terminal mechanical breakdown. Alas, the emasculated killjoy Karl was far from impressed, and no great marketing initiative seems to have been taken as a result of her achievements.

Daimler and Maybach perhaps benefited from the fact that Benz had prepared the market ground. Because they first concentrated their efforts on superior engine design and developed their unit in a home-made motor cycle, the first Daimler engine revved three times as fast as Benz's and featured such *avant-garde* technical features as inlet-over-exhaust valve mechanisms and hot-tube ignition. The latter was to disappear as electrical ignition gained reliability in years to come, although the valve arrangements remained fundamentally unchanged for many years. However, Daimler's advanced engine was mounted in a very unsophisticated carriage chassis. This horseless carriage image was thrown off to some extent with the introduction of the revised Daimler Stahlrad in 1889, but even that was little more than a quadricycle, albeit promisingly equipped with a new, innovative, low-mounted Vee-twin engine giving 1.6hp at 700rpm.

## THE IMPORTANCE OF FRANCE

Unlike Benz, Daimler had the benefit of being able to sell engines (as well as national patent rights for them), instead of only complete cars in these early years, and his connections from his time with Otto at Deutz also proved useful. One of these was the French lawyer Edouard Sarazin, who became Daimler's agent in Paris in 1886. Sarazin made arrangements for the ambitious saw-manufacturing company Panhard-Levassor to build the Daimler engine in France, a country which was to take to the automobile invention with incomparable enthusiasm. The following year Sarazin died but, according to the motoring writer Cyril Posthumus, during his last hours on Christmas Day 1887 Sarazin urged his wife: 'Keep working with Daimler – nobody today has any conception of the enormous potential of his patents.' Madame Sarazin did, succeeding her husband as Daimler's French agent, taking a Daimler engine to Panhard-Levassor for them to make patterns, and so starting the French motor industry.

Benz's first customer was almost certainly a Frenchman, too. Emile Roger was so impressed with Benz's machine in 1888 that he obtained the right to sell Benz cars exclusively in France. But after arranging to build the cars in Paris as the Roger-Benz, Roger seemed no more able to sell the cars than Benz had been. It was another three years before real sales began to take place in Paris, the Frenchman blaming the problem on the fact that the Benz car had only three wheels. In 1893 Benz built a four-wheeled car.

## LEON SERPOLLET, FINEST EUROPEAN EXPONENT OF THE STEAM CAR, STARTS BUSINESS

The Frenchman Leon Serpollet's steam motors and boilers, and particularly his cars, are worthy of special mention. Serpollet was one of the very few manufacturers to make a real success of steam power in an automobile and his cars were extremely fast. At the turn of the century the impressively streamlined Serpollets often out-performed cars powered by 'explosions' (a term which rather quaintly identified the miracle of the internal-combustion engine). On 19th April 1902 *The Autocar* reported: 'Serpollet pulverised all previous records by covering the flying kilometre at the phenomenal rate of 75mph. It is difficult to imagine how this performance can be beaten, for it seems to represent the maximum at which a driver is capable of steering a vehicle, and Serpollet was quite pale when he got down from his car.' Little did the correspondent comprehend how that record would rise to 121 1/2 mph in just three years with Marriott at the wheel of the successful American steam car, the Stanley, such was the rate of technical advance at the time. Nevertheless, the capable, pretty and surprisingly practical Serpollet was the only popular steamer among serious European motorists who could afford perhaps any car they wanted. Alas, when Serpollet died in 1907, his company died with him.

His new Viktoria sold 45 models in the first year – a considerable improvement.

France was a vibrant, ambitious, highly energetic country at the end of the 19th century, and the coming together of inventors and industrialists at the 1889 World's Fair had far-reaching consequences for the infant automobile industry. Both Benz and Daimler demonstrated their cars there, and by the end of the fair the international motor industry had two new manufacturers to add to its number – Panhard Levassor, which decided to start making cars of its own using the Daimler engine, and Peugeot.

The successful French industrialist Armand Peugeot sampled the Daimler Stahlrad at the fair. Already a good business associate of Panhard Levassor, he agreed to buy Daimler engines (three at first) for use in a car of his own design. Significantly, Peugeot had previously been experimenting with a steam-car design using the highly acclaimed Serpollet engine and boiler, but he remained unconvinced of steam's practicality in the light of Daimler's and Benz's achievements. Peugeot went on to build France's first car in 1890, and Panhard Levassor offered theirs the following year.

For perhaps 15 years to come the French, and Panhard Levassor in particular, led the world in mass automobile development.

### THE RESTRICTIONS IN BRITAIN...

After the 1889 World's Fair, the story of the automobile and its pioneers becomes enormously complex, and it was over the following decade that the industry became established in what are now, with the exception of Japan, the principal car-producing nations. But while the pioneering inventors in France and Germany set about improving the commercial automobile, Britain was making little progress.

The cause was the Light Locomotives on Highways Act, otherwise known as the Locomotives Act or the Red Flag Act. This ghastly piece of legislation was first laid down in 1865 and enforced a speed limit of 4mph on machine-powered vehicles (reducable to 2mph at the whim of local government committees). By way of self-regulation, it was also necessary to have a footman carrying a red flag in front of the vehicle and, for reasons never made clear, the vehicle had to have three drivers aboard it. This huge legal obstacle to the early British motorist (for the Act remained substantially unchanged until 1896) was apparently brought about by the environmental problem of Britain's pitiful roads. The coming of the Age of

Steam had led to the demise of fast horse-drawn postal and transport services, and Britain's once excellent roads had fallen into disrepair. Rather than improve them during an era when the railways looked likely to solve the nation's future transport problems, the government simply decided to discourage the public from using them.

The Red Flag Act certainly did that. It made motoring in Britain virtually impossible and put a huge dampener on the British people's ingenuity in designing a car of their own. What was the point, when the inventor could neither develop it nor sell it? No car of any kind existed in England before 1890, and barely half-a-dozen were known in this country as late as 1895. Apart from the Englishman Frederick Lanchester's prototype, all successful models in Britain were imported by pioneer enthusiasts like Frederick Simms, the Hon Evelyn Ellis, S.F. Edge, C.S. Rolls and Sir David Saloman: men of status and influence who broke the law with discretion.

Some assumed that the law wouldn't always remain unchanged. Among them was Frederick Simms (who already knew Daimler through his

*The Australian-born S.F. Edge is on his way to winning the 1902 Gordon Bennett race on the famous green 30hp Napier.*

### THE LANCHESTER: BRITAIN'S FIRST SUCCESSFUL FOUR-WHEEL, PETROL-FUELLED AUTOMOBILE

Britain's earliest cars were Benz-based and appeared in 1895 from the Knight and Petter companies, but neither was a notable success (although John Knight can probably be credited with the first run of a British petrol-fuelled car on the King's Highway). Frederick Lanchester's 1895 car was fundamentally of his own design and astonishingly ahead of its time. This one-cylinder, air-cooled motor even sported disc brakes (which he patented in 1902), the likes of which did not appear on a production road car until Jaguar employed them in their C-type in the 1950s. They are, of course, commonplace on cars today.

*Where our motor industry began: the Daimler works where Britain's first cars were made in 1896.*

family business in Hamburg). He became a director of the Daimler company and thereby secured Daimler's patents for all countries in the British Empire. He formed the Daimler Motor Syndicate in 1893. In 1895 the entrepreneur Harry Lawson attempted to take over the British motor industry outright – before anyone had made a single car – by buying all the patents that would be useful for automobile production in Britain (including the Daimler patents from Simms). In doing so, Lawson formed the British Motor Syndicate.

### ... AND THE ADVANCES IN FRANCE

While Britain struggled to get started, Peugeot and Panhard Levassor were making huge advances. As early as 1891 a Peugeot covered around a thousand almost trouble-free miles in support of the Paris-Brest cycle race; two years later René Panhard gave his young son a 3.5hp Panhard Levassor for his 20th birthday and he promptly drove in it from Paris to Marseille, mountains included, over a six-day period. In 1885 *Le Petit Journal* staged an 80-mile trial from Paris to Rouen and back, which was inevitably a race, and although the steam pioneer and gentleman of fashion, the Comte de Dion, won in his steam-drawn landau, the trial showed great promise for the cars powered by internal-combustion engines – all of them finished.

Indeed, despite de Dion's win, the first prize was awarded jointly to Panhard and Peugeot for their innovative Daimler-engined entries. Significantly, half the members of the steam-powered field broke down, and none of the entries powered by less conservative devices – ranging from bizarre pendulums and electro-pneumatics (!) to air and gravity – so much as reached the start.

With such socialites as the Comte de Dion, Chevalier René de Knyff and Baron Zuylen de Nyevelt involved, the French went on to stage the world's first official motor race in June 1895. This event encompassed a 732-mile thrash running from Bordeaux to Paris and back. Twenty-two cars competed, and Emile Levassor won in just over 48 hours on his new Panhard Levassor powered by Maybach's all-new 3hp Daimler engine. That race was naturally held on open public roads, complete with pedestrians, carts, wagons, dogs and chickens, just as virtually all competitive motor sport events were in France until 1903. In England, with the automobile effectively outlawed, enthusiasts and would-be motorists, inventors, investors and industrialists could do little except file for soon-to-be-obsolete patents and read about foreign progress, as reported in the new British motoring magazine, *The Autocar*.

**EMANCIPATION DAY**

Sir David Saloman, an energetic and keen pioneering motorist, was immensely concerned about the Red Flag Act and its detrimental effect on Britain's standing in the burgeoning word of the motor car. He was a successful inventor himself, having built an electric car as early as 1874, and after consulting like-minded friends he set about organising exhibitions country-wide to educate the public about the need for the motor car. These were supported by a huge PR campaign, including lectures and pamphlet despatch. The scale of the task was enormous – 56,000 letters were written in the first 12 months alone – but the result, carefully steered by colleagues in the House of Commons, was a revision of the Act. The first day of the new legislation was 14th November 1896: Emancipation Day. A new 14mph speed limit was in place, albeit with the usual nod to local government boards allowing them to reduce it to 12mph where they saw fit. At long last the British automobile industry could get motoring.

**THE FIRST ISSUE OF THE AUTOCAR**

The first issue of *The Autocar* appeared on 2nd November 1895. Its editor, Henry Sturmey, had previously founded *The Cyclist* magazine at the age of 22. Sturmey, being primarily a Somerset schoolmaster, insisted the magazine should be called *The Autocar*; he regarded the word 'automobile' both inappropriate and an unacceptable Americanism, as it derived from both the Latin and the Greek. *The Autocar* was a brave publishing initiative and *The Sketch* reviewed the latest arrival on the bookstalls with ridicule: '*The Autocar* is the name of the newest weekly. It is published in the interests of the mechanically-propelled road carriage. What next?' In its early days *The Autocar* was an invaluable organ for the pro-motoring lobby and rapidly grew in circulation and stature. The magazine continues to thrive today as *Autocar* magazine and remains the most successful weekly motoring journal of all.

**WALTER C. BERSEY, THE LAST MOTORIST TO BE SUMMONED FOR SPEEDING BEFORE EMANCIPATION DAY**

Walter C. Bersey was a key early motorist and designer of electric cars and omnibuses. He was also the last to be summoned before the Locomotives Act was revised in 1896 to allow a new 12–14mph speed limit. Suitably enough, Bersey was summoned on two counts: once for not having a footman preceding his car at a distance of 20 yards, and secondly because he did 'unlawfully drive a certain locomotive, to wit, a motor car, through a certain town at a greater speed than 2 miles per hour'.

*Above: This picture was allegedly taken the day before Emancipation Day in an Islington hall. An impressive spread of Daimlers and a lone Benz (flanked by various powered-cycles) prepare to make history.*

*Right: Messrs Hewetson and Arnold outside the Brighton Metropole after finishing the Emancipation Run on 14th November 1896.*

Foreseeing this historic occasion, Harry Lawson, already owner of the British Motor Syndicate and chairman of his own club, The Motor Club, made the most of his influential position to organise a celebration motor drive from London to Brighton. The run attracted 38 cars from France, America and Germany. Lawson drove the Bordeaux-to-Paris-winning Panhard Levassor. As the hosting Earl of Winchilsea ceremonially tore up a red flag at the Whitehall start, so motoring in Britain began – in a fashion. With the nation's magistrates decidedly anti-automobile, and a police force so zealous that no motorist venturing over the new speed limits, even for one moment, could risk escape without a fine, Emancipation Day was at best only a start for the shackled British motor industry. Nevertheless, the London-to-Brighton run is celebrated each November to this day, and is the oldest motoring event in the world, with around 400 pre-1905 automobiles starting in a convoy from Hyde Park.

## BRITAIN GETS STARTED

Britain had much catching up to do. In France the industry comprised numerous important makes, among them such great names as Peugeot and Panhard Levassor, De Dion-Bouton, Léon-Bollée, Delahaye, Rochet-Schneider, Berliet and Mors, many of which were to be central to the world motor business for many years to come. Pioneers in Belgium, Switzerland, Italy and Spain, and numerous individuals in America, were already manufacturing cars to some degree by Emancipation Day, many using Daimler's and Benz's principles, if not their patents. Ironically, only Germany boasted no more all-new manufacturers by 1896, although Friedrich Lutzmann made Benz's four-wheelers; his company later became Opel cars, but that

*London's Royal Agricultural Hall played host to the first London motor show in 1898. And what a motley selection of machinery was on offer! The National Motor Show, incidentally, staged at Crystal Palace, was an early exhibition rival.*

## THE RISE AND FALL OF HARRY LAWSON

It's very easy to be prejudiced against Harry Lawson, who seems to have been something of a self-styled hero and whose determination to get rich quick got the better of his otherwise astute business sense. He was, however, responsible for launching Britain's motor industry with an exceptional energy, having organised The Motor Club, The British Motor Syndicate and the Emancipation Run before revised legislation allowed motoring to establish itself in Britain. *The Autocar* made the highly valid point that it was much easier to have the Red Flag Act repealed when the British motor industry existed but was unable to manufacture because of it. In other words, the existence of the British Motor Syndicate was a far more effective political lever than the moanings of a handful of wealthy sportsmen who wanted to be allowed to drive faster. Unfortunately, Lawson was greedy, selfish and ruthless. He threw his financial weight around, prosecuting anyone else who tried to make a car in Britain. The joint authors of the book *The Automobile – the First Century* describe Lawson as little more than 'a squatter on the freehold of other men's ideas'.

was in 1898. The Germans may have fathered the automobile in the first place, but they were not the most enthusiastic of manufacturers or buyers.

Harry Lawson, effectively the owner of the British motor industry, was now well placed to make his second fortune from the motor business, having already made his first from the cycle industry. He floated his various companies and raised millions of pounds, which he then lost, his patents proving quickly obsolete. Two important Motor Club executives, Frederick Simms and Harrington Moore, promptly disowned Lawson, and in December 1897 they were instrumental in forming the Automobile Club – an independent body formed solely to represent the interests of the motorist.

After the Automobile Club de France, the Automobile Club is the second-oldest motoring organisation in the world and, following Royal patronage in 1907, it became commonly known as the RAC, just as it is today.

The new Automobile Club was a hotbed of pioneering spirit and keen co-operation. It was an

## PETER FALCONER REMEMBERS – THE CONDITION OF EARLY ROADS

*'The only vehicle at my aunt's rectory in Somerset was a governess cart in which she used to take us for drives. We would visit local farms to buy produce, perhaps some cheese, and you would be amazed if you saw a car. If you did, it was bound to be the local squire. He used to drive like a lunatic. He was a bachelor squire, in the true tradition of the type, and he used to tear around. If you heard him coming you took to the hedgerows just in time for him to steam by doing a good 45 miles per hour, because he had quite nice cars.*

*'The dust was a great problem on the roads. If a car went by it took a long time for the dust to settle and all the surrounding greenery and blackberry bushes would be covered with a film of it. Even later when roads were being improved, the problem persisted in the remoter parts of England. You knew there was a car say a mile ahead, simply by all the dust flying. It was impossible to get close simply because as soon as you were within 50 yards of the car the atmosphere was an impenetrable fog. Very often if other road users saw a car coming they would pull off and wait until the dust had settled. And you could smell them after they'd gone by, because they all went along with a cloud of blue smoke coming out.*

*'The roads were improved when crushed stone was steam rolled into them, at least in our vicinity. Then there were the little men with hammers who used to hammer up the local limestone and fill in the many pot-holes. But up the middle of the road there were always the leavings from the horses that used the road. The result was that in the summer there were flies, thousands of flies. That's one of my main memories of the walks I was taken on up to Nailsworth – hundreds of thousands of flies.'*

inspired organisation that allowed the British to make up lost ground fast. At its heart was its secretary Claude Johnson who, in addition to instigating useful daily services to motorists (lists of petrol supply points, for example), organised Britain's first major motor show in 1898 and the important 1000 Mile Trial in 1900. The trial intro-duced motor cars to the general public for the first time and showed them to be useful, practical and reliable. Of the 65 entrants who left London for Scotland and back, 23 finished the course, which did much to promote the right image of the automobile in Britain.

*Some rapid tyre changing for Edge (kneeling) on his way to second place in the inaugural 1000-Mile Trial. The car was owned by Mrs Mary Kennard.*

Now that the Brits were per-mitted to drive their cars at a practical speed, so a market readily developed. But the new demand brought with it all sorts of problems: there were no chauffeurs, driving teachers, mechanics or experts. There was little petrol distribution, the roads were dreadful and breakdowns inevitable for all but the shortest trips. Matters were made worse in England because, until British-made cars (notably Napiers, Lanchesters and Wolseleys) became more readily available after the turn of the century, motorists were left with little option but to buy foreign. Manufacturers were notoriously unhelpful once they had sold the car and an out-of-sight-out-of-mind philosophy seemed to be commonplace among them. Cars didn't come so much with handbooks as with instructions and, with complicated and often inconsistent starting procedures, the pioneer motorist needed more than a good sense of humour in order to live with his or her new acquisition.

Anthony Bird, writing in *The Autocar* in 1973, tells the story of one typical pioneer motorist's misadventure. Mr J.A. Koosen of Southsea – a characteristically enthusiastic but ill-informed customer – bought a Lutzmann in November 1895 because, he said, his wife had 'liked the look of the thing'. Conveniently, it seemed, the Lutzmann was supplied with a letter, detailing the starting pro-cedure of the motor. It simply involved lifting the

## THE 1000 MILE TRIAL

In April 1900 Lord Northcliffe and Claude Johnson of the Automobile Club staged the first 1000 Mile Trial. This was certainly the most serious, the best organised, and the most convincing public relations exercise the pioneer motorists in Britain had yet devised. The route would take 65 cars on a triangular trip, taking in many British cities between London, Edinburgh and Bristol. Not only was it a reliability and speed competition, attracting as it did all the latest models (including S.F. Edge driving the first Napier on its maiden journey) but it also did an enormous amount to demonstrate to the British public just how useful the new automobile invention was. The Automobile Club reported: 'In the cities and towns, the footpaths and roads have been so densely crowded with spectators that only the narrowest passage remained through which the motor vehicles had to pass...' The police seemed to share with the public a keen enjoyment in seeing vehicles speeding at thirty miles an hour, and sympathised with the rebukes which the crowd addressed to drivers who failed to go at top speed.

engine lid and turning the flywheel. Koosen went about the exercise with appropriate zeal, but after several hours his only accomplishment was to wear through his gardening gloves. Ten days passed and, despite the help of local engineers, no further progress was made until someone suggested that a mysterious liquid might be required to fuel the machine. Mrs Koosen's diary celebrated: 'Motor *went*, with Benzoline. Awfully pleased.'

### MOTORPHOBIA

Whilst the problems of buying and running an automobile were, if costly and inconvenient, at least within the powers of the motorist to control, the problems created by the police and general public were not. As Raymond Flower and Michael Wynn Jones acknowledge in their excellent book *One Hundred Years of Motoring*: 'Many far-reaching inventions have been greeted initially with suspicion, apprehension or abuse. But the depth of hostility aroused by the early automobiles was remarkable in itself. The pioneers came to expect it and classified each outburst as another manifestation of the malaise they called motorphobia.'

Claude Johnson, the creator of the 1000 Mile Trial, was the first secretary of the RAC and later managing director of Rolls-Royce. He reminisced in *The Autocar* in 1916: 'It is difficult to imagine any country in which a prophecy that the horse was to be driven off the road by mechanical vehicles could be more unwelcome than in this country. In this kingdom the horse, the coachman, the groom, the carriage maker, the horse breeder and the horse trainer have for centuries been considered to be almost the backbone of the country's existence.'

One can but empathise with the common man who may hardly have seen or even heard of a motor car. The devices were frightening, noisy and kicked up huge quantities of dust from the road. They may well have threatened ordinary people's livelihoods and, because cars were expensive to buy and to run, they were invariably owned and driven by, literally, the filthy rich. The automobile was a new weapon in the class wars of the turn of the century, and the warring parties met on the King's Highway – the 'haves' versus the 'have-nots'.

Unfortunately for the new motorists, police officers were numbered among the 'have-nots', and with their worthy allies, the local magistrates, 'the law' was keen to round up the toffs quickly, and the anti-motoring lobby gathered great momentum. 'There is an embittered feeling in the general public against all persons who use motor cars which, as a dangerous class feeling, is, perhaps, without parallel in modern times', stated the president of the Local Government Board.

*Nothing less than Baron de Stern's garden party held in Strawberry Hill (near Twickenham) in 1900... with a fine spread of motors. At that time, motoring was a pastime which only the very wealthy could enjoy.*

*Left: Believe it or not, this motoring mishap resulted in the deaths of Edwin Sewell and Major Ritchie. These were Britain's first recorded motor-deaths. The scene is their broken Coventry-Daimler on Grove Hill, Harrow, July 1899.*

*Below: The start of the anti-motoring lobby!*

THE POLICE ACT.
Reckless Driving. Sec. 54.
(b) A police constable may stop & take into custody any person who drives furiously. · · · ·

*Right: As early motorists and the established road users learnt to share the available space, road accidents became common, and the motorist usually got the blame.*

*Below: A lovely Edwardian Humber advert showing a fanciful supremacy over the speed trappers. Wildly ambitious claims by manufacturers at the time ('No Dust. No Noise') were generally wholly unjustifiable.*

The Hon Charles Rolls, soon to become one of the most important figures in the history of the automobile when he went into business with Henry Royce to make Rolls-Royce cars, was an eminent pioneer motorist. In a speech given near his home town in Monmouth, Rolls recounted with pride the adventures of a trip he made to his home from Cambridge University at the end of the 1896 winter term in his 3½hp Peugeot.

Knowles, his friend and passenger on that trip, recalled Rolls as saying: 'But in the country, on the other hand, when the car was moving, every other man climbed up a tree or telegraph pole to get out of the way, every woman ran away across the fields, every horse jumped over the wall and every butcher's cart that was left at the side of the road with the tailboard down, bolted off, scattering various parts of animals along the road.' Rolls went on: 'On our trip here I even saw some old ladies jump the wall of a churchyard. We passed a field with farm labourers working near the edge of the road; the whole company ran away at full speed across the big field!'

If such childish boasts seem incredible coming from one as respected as Rolls, then be sure they were typical the motoring world over. A famous De Dion advert in 1899 featured a colour illustration of a speeding open De Dion, its driver watching his lady passenger (rather than the road) as she sat for all the world to see, dress lowered, breast-feeding her infant. Apparently unaware of anything else around him, the driver is also running over two terrified pigs and narrowly missing a horse-drawn cart (significantly driven by a pale-faced Eastern immigrant, rather than a Westerner), the horse rearing up in terror. This advertisement tells so many stories, but the proudly-promoted arrogance of the driver (flaunted, it must be assumed, to appeal to all aspiring De Dion drivers) is blatant.

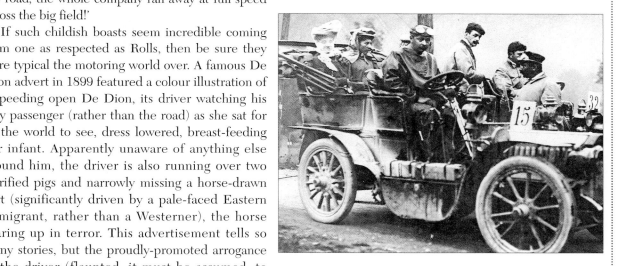

*Above: Ladies had it tough when it came to motoring. They seldom drove and usually sat high in the back of the motor, heads wrapped in gauze to keep the billowing dust out. Looking glamorous was the least of their priorities.*

Flower's and Wynn Jones' writings, which are sources of many splendid reminiscences from the pioneer period, recall a tale told by S.F. Edge, the pioneer British racing driver and future sole distributor for the important English Napier car. Edge was driving through Crawley on a cold winter's night in 1900 when he was hit on the head by a rock. Spying a yokel in his lamps, he gave chase over two fields before capturing the supposed culprit. He then stripped him to his pants and shoes, depositing the rest of his clothes at the next village. One can imagine Edge recounting this story with guffawing pride, without considering that such a demeaning action would have done nothing to help the motorists' cause. Alas, extreme sexism, racism, arrogance and selfishness seemed a hallmark of the man over the wheel.

In 1902 – the same year that motorists campaigned for the abolition of all speed limits (the limit was raised to only 20mph the next year) – *Car*

*Illustrated* made a telling editorial comment: 'Do not a good many of the complaints about the speed of motor cars on the road arise from the human tendency to jealousy at seeing a vehicle going faster than you are and passing you? Any driver of a hansom, if another passes him, will whip up his horse and endeavour to re-pass.' The writer continued: 'A man with a fast-trotting horse, who has hitherto been king of the road, is now completely overshadowed by even the most modest motor.'

On the very same page in *Car Illustrated* is another comment, about the emergence in America of cranks who threatened to shoot drivers breaking the speed limit. This might have been an unreasonable fate for the driver of the quite common runaway car unable to maintain its speed down a hill. Police often regarded such motorists as easy prey, and the writer suggests a notice that would seem appropriate to the circumstances: 'Don't shoot the driver, he is doing his best to stop.' But you can't blame the Americans when the French were doing the same thing. In around 1897 a Monsieur Hugues le Roux was apparently run down by a motorist in the Bois de Boulogne going 'at the speed of an express train'. In a furious letter to the Paris Prefect of the Police he described motorists as 'mad dogs' before reasonably informing the Prefect that he intended to shoot anyone driving a car in future.

### THE DRIVING EXPERIENCE

The taming of the automobile must have been extraordinarily challenging for pioneering motorists. Even if such people had seen an automobile before, or ridden in one on occasion, they would still have probably had no driving or mechanical experience to draw on. The fastest speed at which the new motorist could ever have travelled at that time (except by train) would have been around 12mph, and that speed was achieved only by the fit rider of a well-oiled bicycle.

Consider, too, the likelihood of these early journeys being undertaken on very poor, rutted road surfaces (for tarmaced roads were very rare in those days). These either threw up clouds of dust in dry weather (which damaged the car's exposed mechanicals as readily as it irritated the passengers) or became boggy and slippery in wet weather, promoting lethal skidding and side-slip on the skinny wheels and tyres of the day. If the car in question was an early veteran, and therefore not fitted with pneumatic tyres, the ride would have been wholly atrocious and the steering wheel would have wrenched viciously on the hands. Then again, if pneumatics were fitted, punctures would have been almost inevitable, and tyres were not at all easy to change.

Of course, early cars had no windscreens, let alone windscreen wipers, and no heaters. They had dreadful lighting and only occasionally roofs, which operated more as dust shelters than as serious weather protection.

Add to all these factors the poor fuel-distribution network (bottles from chemists and the occasional grocer or pub were the best one could hope for); the high chances of a mechanical breakdown occurring (yet without the range of back-up services that exist today); the probability of an altercation with the police – and some idea of the early motorists' pioneering spirit can be imagined.

But even before the fun and games of motoring could commence, the new motorist had to work out how to operate the automobile. There were no driving tests. Written instructions, if provided in intelligible English, would have been brief in the extreme. So he or she simply had to attempt to control the new acquisition as much by trial and error as through any formal instruction. It would have been easier, of course, if the new motorist had seen another car started or driven, but the fact remained that many early automobile makers designed control systems which bore little relation to their rivals'. Therefore experience of one car's controls may not have been applicable to another.

Fortunately, there was often a common theme to car controls: the device for steering; the little – and confusing – levers for the engine throttle, ignition, and valve pressure; the long external lever for the rear-wheel brake, the foot-pedal for the transmission brake and the short, thick lever for gear selection. What is more, all of these needed to be frequently used or adjusted in an ever-changing choreography which, when the gesticulations of turn signals were also required, was a fearsome, frantic challenge.

Consider the complications, for example, of a common slowing-down-to-corner manoeuvre: with the slowing of the car on the throttle lever together with the brake pedal, the ignition also needed to be adjusted along with the valve pressure... while the clutch was disengaged, the gear was changed, the wheel turned, the handsignals were given... and all this was casually accomplished while the driver was looking where he or she was going. Of course, the expert driver would learn all manner of short cuts, but becoming expert was potentially – and usually – a hazardous business.

Then again, the joys of controlling the car could only be realised if the vehicle in question could be roused in the first place. That usually involved the opening of the bonnet, the filling of the radiator with coolant, the retarding of the ignition, the weakening of the valve pressure, the setting of the throttle, the putting of the gearbox in neutral, the opening of the fuel valve, the priming of the carburettor, the closing of the bonnet, the insertion and swinging of the starting handle (whilst being careful not to suffer its wrist-breaking backlash when the car started), the advancing of the ignition, the increasing of the valve pressure...

*What the devil...!*
*A Towcester church appears to have been taken over by the burgeoning motor trade. It's around 1903, and the newly-converted sit menacingly on board a pair of Daimlers and an ever-so-formidable Mercedes.*

*'Pine! Change that tyre!'
Lord Northcliffe (in the
fur) observes his faithful
chauffeur, Pine, making
his trousers dirty
somewhere on the road
to Pau in 1908. The
chances are that Pine
wouldn't have driven
very much, and was
only on board for the
grubbier tasks.*

From the mid-1890s to the beginning of the the First World War, the car was technically refined almost beyond recognition. Speeds that would be considered fast today were achievable by the better sporting models, while returning good fuel consumptions. Well-engineered sports cars were able to return 15-18mpg from perhaps 4.5-litre engines, while refined slow-revving cars like the superb 7-litre Rolls-Royce Ghost could achieve around 20mpg on a run. The light car, which was becoming established by 1910, could frequently return fuel consumption approaching 30mpg.

Fuel availability, too, was becoming more widespread, and petrol was now generally available in 2-gallon cans (and at the equivalent of less than 10p a gallon) from a wide variety of sources, not least from the new business enterprise suddenly making its appearance in many villages throughout the land – the garage.

Three or four-speed gear-changing was a vast improvement on the early methods, but in reality gear-changing was still a chore that many drivers did their best to avoid, either labouring the car in too high a gear for the speed, or revving the car too high through a reluctance to change up. While the speed capabilities of the car had grown enormously, the limit remained 20mph, which gave the police enormous scope for speed trapping on a military scale, which, of course, they did.

There were fewer levers on the steering column of an Edwardian car – one built between 1905 and 1918 – than on earlier models. The throttle was now more likely to be a pedal on the floor, possibly situated between the brake pedal and the clutch. The brake pedal still tended to operate only the transmission brake; the outside lever was still responsible for those at the rear and used only in emergencies. The fuel tap on the Edwardian car still had to be opened and closed at the beginning and end of trips, but now the petrol tank had to be pressurised by hand-pump before the car was started.

Instrumentation on pre-First World War cars was still minimal, but a row of lubrication glasses dominated the dashboard equipment like test tubes in a rack, showing that all was well with the lubricative works. A speedometer may have been fitted, but oil pressure and electrical gauges generally had yet to arrive. Tachometers were very rare fittings. Dashboard-mounted fuel gauges were unheard of.

Road conditions were generally little better than a decade before, and one might have thought that a closed car would be the popular choice, if only to protect from the weather and dirt. In fact, the weight and loftiness of closed cars frequently undermined their road manners. Besides, this was an era when the thrill of the motoring experience was still craved by drivers and passengers alike: the closed car, which was yet to gain a heater and so be of luxurious consequence in the winter, was just plain boring by comparison. Open cars were therefore still the norm and their weather equipment was much improved. Windscreens were now common, although the mechanical windscreen wiper had yet to arrive, drivers relying on either a strip of felt mounted on a swivelling metal arm or the more natural abilities of a fresh-cut potato to clear a dirty windscreen. Heavy rains, which could swamp the abilities of even the boldest King Edward, could demand the opening or lowering of the screen to allow for a clearer view.

Apart from the frequency of punctures, the effort required to swing on the starting handle of a car was perhaps the biggest deterrent to the prospective early motorist. It was the Anglicised Australian S.F. Edge, ever the man in front in motoring matters, who marketed the first electric starter for an English production automobile in 1913, and this development made motoring much more attractive to the masses and to ladies in particular (even if a couple of swings on the starter handle were still recommended before using the self-starter on a cold engine).

Another piece of technical wizardry made available thanks to the advance of reliable electrics was a new lighting system for cars. The earliest electric automobile lights appeared in or around 1910 and were much safer and more reliable than the acetylene-fuelled items they replaced. Acetylene gas was produced by drip-feeding water onto carbide crystals packed into canisters. The gas produced was then piped to open flame lamps. While the acetylene burned with a certain brilliance, the reflectors required to throw the light forward onto the road seldom lasted long. Such romantic but limited lighting, together with the acetylene's constant explosive threat, rendered night-time motoring a hazardous business. A full moon and a cloud-free sky were desirable early night-driving aids, at least until electric lighting became established.

With so many complications and hazards presented, to say nothing of the laborious maintenance of bodywork and mechanics required, it is little wonder that the owners of Veteran cars (built to 1905) and then Edwardian ones came to demand help in their daily motoring. And so a new and extremely popular post became available in many well-to-do households: that of the chauffeur.

### IT'S A CHAUFFEUR'S LIFE

A glance through the classified adverts in a 1906 copy of the weekly journal *The Autocar* gives an insight into who and what a chauffeur was. Under the heading 'Drivers Disengaged' are more than two dozen adverts from hopeful young men eager to get over the wheel. Most immediately obvious are the advertisers' ages: the majority are in their mid-twenties, and some in

*Like father like son, and who could blame the child? Being a chauffeur was a terrific job for a young working-class man. How else could he hope to get his hands on a car of any kind, let alone this c.1908 Star? Adventure was guaranteed and the pay was good, too.*

*The chauffeur shares his boss's picnic. It's 1906, it's a Vauxhall, and there's a lot of wine on the running board!*

their teens. Mr Dansea of Walworth is a typical advertiser. His advertisement reads: 'Driver-Mechanic. 25, experienced, repairs, excellent references from last and previous berths, clean licence, any petrol car, town or country, quick at tyres.' Others specify the makes of car they wish to drive, while under the 'Drivers Recommended' section Captain Whetherly of Egerton Gardens in London advertises his 'reliable, honest and sober' chauffeur for employment on a Mercedes 40 mount. Nice work if you could get it!

The chauffeur's job was a terrific one – there was no doubt about that – particularly if you were lucky enough to be employed by an exceptionally wealthy individual who knew his autos from his perambulators. After all, how else could a servant (for that's what a chauffeur was) hope to get his hands on the most exotic and exciting device that man had so far devised? For most it was dream enough to ride in an automobile, but actually to drive one (and an expensive one at that) and to

## GEORGE LLEWELYN REMEMBERS – EARLY COUNTRY DRIVING

*'We lived in Little Ness, a small village community in those days, in a quiet atmosphere. If you'd got a bicycle then you were well off. There was no bus service to the villages, and the nearest station was 2 or 3 miles away. Instead all the people relied on a horse-drawn wagonette that took people to and from Shrewsbury, with all their produce.*

*'The local children used to stop and watch if there was a car standing. And they'd probably wait quite a time to see it start. The local farmer had a Model T Ford and so did the doctor. I was eight years old then, when the first car came to our village. It must have been 1913.*

*'Motorists weren't always resented by the horse-drawn fraternity. They realised, I think, that motors had come to stay, but drivers would often have to get down to hold the horse if a car went by. It was mostly coachmen who resented the motorists. There was a poem we used to say which went, "Just think of a nice carriage, drawn by a handsome pair; a coachman proud and pompous, with that condescending air; a footman both arms folded, and supercilious mien, a vehicle more dignified, is nowhere to be seen." If you were a coachman you were "someone" in those days, with their cockades worn in their silk hats. But they graduated to the car in the end – became chauffeurs themselves.*

*'The first drive I made of any distance was to take my boss's wife and her friend out to a strawberry tea party at a house in the country... I remember the car had a screen on it, but no side curtains or anything like that. It was quite open and it was a lovely day and I came back from there and I thought, "Well, I've done it at last, I've driven a motor car." And it went on from there, you see.'*

be paid for the privilege was the ultimate job for a working-class motor enthusiast.

Of course, in the earliest days, finding a qualified chauffeur was probably impossible, so rather than lay off the coachman when the new automobile arrived, it was logical to encourage the equestrian in the new magic of motors. Besides, there was every bit as much work to do in the upkeep of the new motor car as there had been with the coach and horses. But while looking after the motor car's coachwork and fittings was a familiar task, driving the mechanical thing was an awesome prospect to the animal-empathising coachman.

Consider the responsibility involved. Most of us have ridden in a modern car driven on modern roads by a modern motorist who has passed a modern driving test, and yet we have been terrified every minute of the trip (let's be honest, every family has a driver like that). Yet despite the seat-gripping terror of such an occasion, the chances of injury or death are probably minimal, even if a bent bumper is a likely keepsake.

Well, just imagine how terrifying it would have been in the Edwardian era, sitting in the passenger seat of an open high-performance tourer that stood taller than a man, perhaps 20 feet long and weighing up to 3 tons, its driver demanding all of 60hp from the big multi-cylinder, mega-litre engine. Imagine the deafening deep exhaust throb, the dust-filled gale about you and the jarring ride from the skinny wheels on the rutted roads. Imagine the sense of trust you had to have in the driver of such a near-brakeless monster as it hurtled and thundered at speeds up to 70mph. Make no mistake, although my specified beast would have been among the more exotic available before the First World War, some of the best cars could roar along at 70mph, and even at half that velocity such trips often represented life on the edge.

After all, the orchestrator of the high drama – the individual in control of the machine and so of the lives of the passengers and the onlooking pedestrians – was the servant up-front in the big armchair wrestling with a wheel the size of a dustbin lid. With the determination of a Gordon Bennett race-winner, this horseman-turned-chauffeur was a self-styled hero of the most lethal kind. He was the highest-paid servant in the household and had a double-breasted, brass-buttoned tunic (probably a lounge jacket after 1910) to boast his all-new status, complete with officer-style hat, jodhpurs and knee-high boots in parade-black leather. Resplendent thus, he would have you believe that he was the best in his business and that his steed was the fastest, most beautiful and most expensive in the land – even if it wasn't quite a Rolls-Royce.

It's true. Before the advent of chauffeuring schools run by up-market motor manufacturers such as Rolls-Royce and Napier, plus the Automobile

*The chauffeur was well placed to have a close relationship with members of his master's family. As Miss Kitty Gordon demonstrates, rarely would staff and employer otherwise get so intimate.*

*This extraordinary picture was taken in 1912 on the occasion of the Earl of Ellesmere's annual chauffeurs' picnic. There are 13 of them. Think of the cost... and that's just for the picnic.*

Club from 1904, chauffeurs learnt their trade by reading instruction sheets, having the odd lesson from a helpful motor dealer, and trial and error. In the early days, when most car owners also drove their motors, the chauffeur was given the more servile role of keeping the car going (starting, stopping, coping with breakdowns and tyre changes, cleaning and maintaining being his principal tasks), but as driving lost its purely sporting image and became more essentially a means of transport, so the chauffeur came to acquire an unprecedented status among the members of the household staff. It was the chauffeur who was trusted to take care of the ladies when on the road and of the mistress on her calling rounds; it was the chauffeur who was privy to the conversations of passengers; it was the chauffeur who knew his employer's travels intimately; and it was the chauffeur who was responsible for the safe and timely transport of loved ones.

Armed with such status and brandishing the keys to the employer's motoring stable (large collections of cars were quite common among the wealthy), it is no wonder that the chauffeur often got rather too big for his knee-boots. As demand for chauffeurs grew they gained a reputation for bad driving, joy-riding, and having ideas far above their stations in life. Flower and Wynn Jones record the following sentiment from an aggrieved correspondent of 1906:

'Much of the horror of motoring is centred in the chauffeur. It is his convenience that has to be consulted, it is he who gives the word to stop and to go on, he who decides that you must sleep at Coventry when you had intended to go on to Shrewsbury. You may not make plans without consulting him; he is ruthless in his discouragements; he spends your money with a fine liberality, and you learn to dread his statement of accounts, presented on the oily page of a notebook. He smokes the vilest known cigarette... he eats and drinks expensively, and at the wayside inns where you put up he monopolises the service.'

The chauffeur's non-driving duties were a good deal less glamorous. *Autocar* magazine reminds us that more than 40 different operations could be involved in a weekly service, and early chain-drive cars required their chains to be regularly boiled in Russian tallow. In the absence of efficient gasket material and dipsticks, not only did mechanical units leak oil profusely but also their oil levels had to be checked by removing their top plates – never less than a laborious task. The many oil leaks caused dirt to cling to the underside of the car on any trip, and with many mechanical items woefully exposed to the elements, cleanliness was essential if the car was to remain reliable.

Most chauffeurs were required to present their vehicles gleaming before journeys, and many a stable was kept with a 'bonnets up' policy, so any random inspection would show how immaculately the works were maintained.

With the enormous quantities of brass and nickel that had to be kept polished, the preparation of a quality Edwardian car for a journey was a full-time job. Small wonder that, once at the wheel, the chauffeur had a tendency to get carried away.

## THE MOTORISTS FIGHT BACK

It would seem incredible today that the national police force could get away with such vindictive methods as they used during the days of the anti-motoring lobby, a period which existed from the day a car first turned a wheel to at least the First World War. Whether the root of the problem lay more in the caddish actions of the toffs with the motors or the jealousies and ignorance of the yokels is a moot point. The fact remains that the public and so the press, the police and so the courts, had little sympathy with the pioneer drivers. *The Times* observed: 'There is no turning a cad into a gentleman, but there is such a thing as making even cads fear the law.' And with such a worthy task to accomplish, the police set to work against the motorist with fanatical zeal.

The coming of the omnibus did much to appease the public, who could not very well deplore the machinations of the motor car when they enjoyed a ride on a bus, and the experiences of the First World War also did much to curb the basic hatred. The newly-designed and built tank, and to a lesser extent other military vehicles, did so much to win the war for Great Britain that the worth of mechanical vehicles could hardly be criticised by those

*The motor bus and charabanc were the common man's usual introduction to motoring, and their popularity was important in the quashing of the anti-motoring lobby. These Milnes-Daimler machines (plus one Straker-Squire on the right) date from around 1905.*

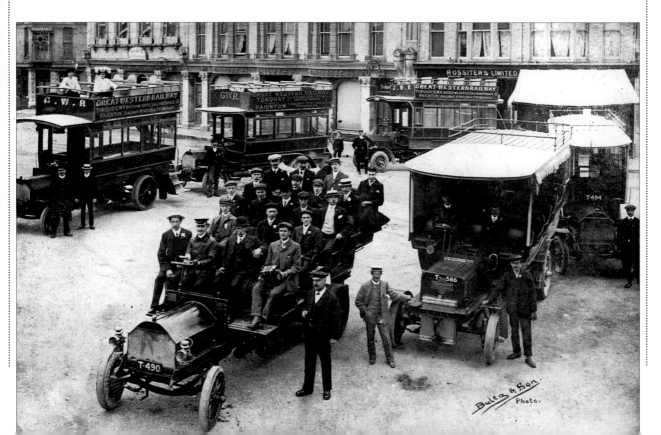

*It's 1907 and the first AA patrols went on duty looking like this. Armed with nothing but cycle clips and a spirited sense of decency, these true knights of the road would patrol in search of police speed traps and then warn oncoming motorists of the dangers ahead.*

who witnessed it. Nevertheless, until the tide of public opinion changed, the motorists could do little but rally their resources against the vindictive armoury of the police, and they did so through forming pressure groups. The most famous, successful and bold of these was the Automobile Association, or AA.

The AA was founded in 1905, having grown out of a cycle patrol organised by the London motor dealers Jarratt and Letts. The patrol was set up to help motorists avoid police speed traps which littered the main roads nationwide. At that time a typical speed trap comprised three policeman squatting in hedgerows or up trees a furlong from one another. As the hapless motorist passed the first policeman, the latter would wave to his two colleagues down the road, being careful that the driver didn't see. The second policeman would then start a watch, stopping it as the car passed a marker. If the car was found to be exceeding the speed limit, which it almost invariably was, then the third policeman would jump from his hideaway and gleefully call a halt. This rather underhand practice was nothing short of legalised highway robbery, and while the muddied police regarded themselves as latter-day Robin Hoods, taking from the rich to give to, presumably, the poor, the motorists saw it as yet another attempt to halt the flow of motoring progress in Britain.

The AA's initiative was a splendidly British jewel of democratic social history: the AA men would bicycle down busy roads spotting police traps before parking their bicycles upstream to warn oncoming drivers of the speed trap ahead. There was nothing illegal in this; the AA was a voluntary organisation of good eggs trying to help those beleaguered chaps with motors. Simple as that. In order to identify themselves AA scouts would wear special armbands and before long they became the heroes of the motoring movement.

Organised with military efficiency, the AA also acquired a salute which, it was carefully explained to motorists, was a polite form of greeting. Motorists who spotted AA scouts, and scouts who spotted motorists, would always salute one another with a militant show of strength and organisation. Not surprisingly, the authorities were less than impressed with the AA's activities, and when it began to look probable that scouts could be arrested for obstructing the course of justice the AA dealt with the problem simply but effectively. They changed their now-traditional saluting techniques so that if an AA scout did not return the salute of a passing motorist, it meant that a speed trap or similar danger lay ahead. Such a passive warning method was simple and ever so legal.

Realising that they were doing an awful lot for the motorist for nothing, the AA then became a serious business, motorists subscribing to the club's services and showing AA badges on the fronts of their cars to allow scouts to ascertain whether a motorist qualified for help. The organisation went from strength to strength, soon offering breakdown, first-aid, navigation and hostelry services. AA boxes containing emergency telephones sprang up along the roadsides, scouts using them as their bases, but eventually members were supplied with keys for their personal access.

In the years to come, with the police offensive largely over, the AA concentrated their efforts on every conceivable service for the motorist, and their success can be quantified in a membership roll claiming 8.6 million names in 1995.

The evolution of the RAC (as the Automobile Club became known after coming under Royal patronage in 1907) was rather less militant and aggressive than that of the AA. None the less, its early members had a very important role to play in representing the motorists' interests among those in government and the legislators. While in due course the RAC also evolved a breakdown and recovery service network of a similar kind to that offered by the AA, the club also became an organising and administrative body for national motorsport. The RAC, too, thrives to this day, and still has its headquarters and gentlemen's club in a superb building in London's Pall Mall, where it has been based since 1911.

## GETTING A GOOD LAWYER

Apart from the good works of the AA, the motorist's only other defence in the war against the police and magistrates was a good lawyer and, expensive though they were, lawyers were often hired by wealthy motorists. T.W. Staplee-Firth KC built up a formidable reputation in the early years as someone who could get a young man with a very fast car out of all kinds of trouble.

According to the author G.R.N. Minchin, writing in 1950, in around 1912 Staplee-Firth even managed to get the great pioneer aviator Gustav Hamel off a five-point summons after Hamel, driving his enormous Weigel racing car, had run into a speed trap on the way back from Brooklands racing circuit and not stopped. Instead of reaching the obstructing policeman he turned right off the road at around 50mph, took to the towpath along the river, and avoided a low bridge by crashing through a hedge and driving across a field before negotiating a wood and smashing through a garden fence to rejoin the road. Being a proper chap, Hamel stopped to offer to pay for the broken fence, but unfortunately the police then passed by and booked

*How to make your poodle hot, bothered and altogether irritable. And I'd wager that motoring for Fi Fi was a mite chilly around the lower leg, too...*

47

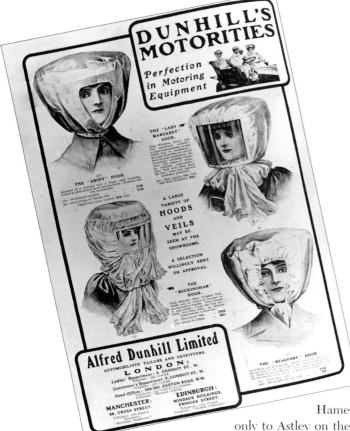

*The selection of fashions that rapidly became available for motorists was astounding, and no outfitters were more prolific or inspired than Dunhill's. Their 'Bobby Finders' slogan ranks among the best in advertising history!*

him while he was negotiating the damages. Staplee-Firth had the case quashed because Hamel had got one of his passengers – another great aviator, Otto Astley – to sit in the driver's seat while he paid for the fence. Knowing Hamel's car, but not Hamel personally, the police spoke only to Astley on the day; Astley did not let on that he'd never driven the car, and Staplee-Firth got the case thrown out accordingly.

### LOOKING THE PART

The motorists' problems with the police couldn't have been made any easier when their dress was taken into consideration. Sitting high up on their automobiles, the early motorists not only appeared to look down on everything about them but also often did so wearing extremely costly clothing. Wealth and privilege seldom came more blatant. In fairness, it *was* necessary to keep driver and passengers warm, dry and dust-tight. These were environmental challenges that simply had to be conquered if motoring wasn't to prove to be a hellish experience.

Such protective clothing was always expensive, usually huge, and invariably covered the face and head to such an extent that both driver and passengers looked like criminals on the run. Hats, visors, fur stoles, lined goggles with hinged nose-pieces, tinted glass and polished metal eye-pieces, silk hoods with liftable transparent shields, gauze veils, woollen coats with astrakhan collars, leggings and breeches, leather and wool blankets, rubber-necked umbrella mackintosh smocks, sheepskin underwear, kid-skin helmets, chamois knickers... you name it, the automotive fashion-conscious tried it and flaunted it.

The scale of the motor-fashion business before the First World War was amazing, with well-established clothiers such as Aquascutum, Burberry, Dunhill and Drykitt all offering a spectacular range. Many looked utilitarian and ungainly but some were truly inspired. In my opinion Dunhill led the British field with *avant garde* motoring fashions which really stood out from the crowd, some smacking of fetishisms only found later in seventies art movies. Unfortunately, the better the look, the more impractical it usually was.

Make no mistake, nothing looked more impressive than a Mercedes driver sitting high up and looking monstrous in his superb Siberian wolf-skin coat, his seal-fur cap and his tinted goggles. Attired in this way, he looked like a true 'king of the road', at least before the drive began. Unfortunately, though, after a short while on the road he might begin to look in a very sorry state indeed, the dry roads impregnating the fur of his coat with dust and dirt, or a wet road giving 'his highness' the heavy, miserable look of a water-logged dog.

The changeable weather in Britain presented the motorist with a particular fashion problem, as what was comfortable for dry weather was probably quite unsuitable for rainy conditions, and vice versa. Leather was criticised because of its unwieldy weight and the fact that it caused the wearer to sweat

*Above: Ladies take to the road in a Peugeot Bébé. The coming of the well-engineered miniature car brought many ladies true freedom of the road for the first time.*

*Left: Lady chauffeurs were very rare, but this picture shows Esther Goodall standing by the 1914 Napier 33 which a Leeds family employed her to drive. Most Edwardian chauffeurs were in their early-to-mid-twenties, and driving such valuable cars was an enormous responsibility.*

*Above: It's the future Queen Mary en famille and at the wheel of a 1905 Panhard. This photo shows the car's enormous size to good effect. 19 people are in the picture yet the car is hardly dwarfed.*

*Right: This is the Hon C.S. Rolls's stand at the 1905 Motor Show in London's Olympia. Rolls had recently met Henry Royce and was so impressed by his car that he agreed to go into partnership with him and to sell the renamed Rolls-Royce cars exclusively.*

badly. Most furs were considered impractical and also heavy, although seal fur was more waterproof and serviceable. Popular waterproofs were made of gaberdine or Aquascutum (the latter having highly prestigious Royal patronage), while tweed and mohair outfits offered warmer protection. In reality, the wet-dry, hot-cold problem was never successfully solved, although many motorists would spend fortunes ascertaining that fact for themselves. The result was a wide and expensive range of distinctly outlandish fashions that demanded a large wallet and an even larger wardrobe.

Ladies had it especially tough, as they had the additional problems of maintaining their hairstyles, complexions and demeanours while still looking as glamorous as possible. It was an impossible challenge, and for more than 20 years the lady motorist suffered intolerably until the closed car and tarmac roads became the norm.

### ROLLS AND ROYCE

By 1903 the world production of motor vehicles was 62,000, and around half came from France. In Britain, progress was slow but sure. S.F. Edge had run the first Napier car in the 1000 Mile Trial of 1900, and the historic partnership of Edge and D. Napier & Son saw the world's first production six-cylinder engine launched in 1904. At that time the Napier was considered to be the finest car in England, but that reputation was soon to be threatened with the arrival of the quintessential Edwardian automobile, the Rolls-Royce.

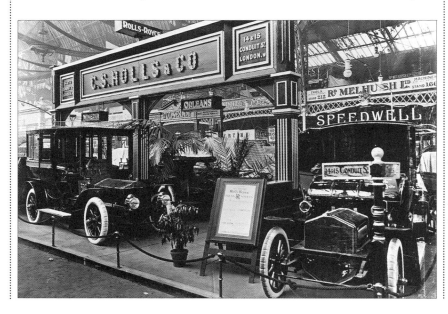

In 1903 Henry Royce was running a company making electrical cranes. He was a motorist and a perfectionist, which accounted for his disliking the build quality and lack of refinement of his French Decauville car. Convinced he could do better, he designed and built the Royce car – a two-cylinder 20hp machine based on the Decauville. He finished the car on 1st April 1904; when he swung the starting handle for the first time it came to life without hesitation and went on to motor its maiden 15-mile journey without missing a beat.

Rolls has already been mentioned in these pages as a pioneer motorist and in 1902 he set up as a garagist operating from Fulham and Mayfair in London. There he specialised in selling French and Belgian cars, but only because, in his opinion, the British had yet to produce something that suited his market. He was not yet very familiar with the new Royce car, but a friend of his, Henry Edmunds, was and eventually persuaded Rolls to travel to Manchester with him to meet Royce. The resulting liaison became one of the most important in the whole of automobile history.

## 1907: THE BEST CAR IN THE WORLD

The Rolls-Royce 40/50 Ghost was a big and beautifully engineered car powered by an understressed 7-litre engine. It was remarkable not so much for its technical innovations as for its unprecedented refinement and flexible performance. Royce designed and built the Ghost – a car that was to remain the best money could buy for nearly two decades – within three years of attempting his first automobile design. Such an achievement was previously unheard-of. Though not designed as a performance car, in 1911 a Ghost tourer successfully drove from London to Edinburgh in top gear, averaging over 24mpg in the process. The following year a Ghost Continental attempted the arduous Alpine Trial in Austria, but the car's gearing was wrong and the team had to return the next year. This they did, winning the event outright without losing any points. A Ghost won again the next year, too, just to make the point! Even today a Ghost will cope with modern traffic conditions economically, reliably and effortlessly, and will deliver its passengers stress-free and refreshed even after a long journey. In the Edwardian years the car was an unrivalled masterpiece, and it gave Rolls-Royce their still unshakeable international reputation as the manufacturers of the best of their kind in the world.

## RALPH LEE REMEMBERS – DEVOTION TO HIS FIRST VINTAGE CAR

'Eventually the great day arrived when I'd got enough money to be able to buy a motor car for myself. I particularly wanted a Peugeot – the baby Peugeot – a little cabriolet two-seater. I'd never seen one, but I'd seen pictures of them and learnt how they worked. Anyway, I heard of one for sale in Northamptonshire. I was living in Surrey and I bought this car and drove it home through London. And I'd never had a driving lesson, or driven a car. I'd learnt it all through books.

'The young enthusiast in those days regarded his machine as an idol. He liked to do everything himself, with his own hands. We'd think nothing of taking the engine to pieces and fitting new pistons, often in the garden because there was no garage, and when it rained you had to rush out and put the tarpaulin over it. I also remember oil everywhere. Of course we didn't have oil seals in those days, so everything used to leak. If you had a reasonable set of tools you could do everything yourself, unlike today. And that was half the fun. Sometimes you'd do a job on the car that wasn't really even necessary, just for the fun of it, or we'd take things to pieces, always trying to get another mile or two out of a gallon of petrol.

'Of course good motor mechanics really knew how to mend anything. It was never a case of ringing up the supplier and getting replacements sent. I remember on one occasion I ran the big ends of my car's engine driving up the Porlock hill. I only had to leave it at the local garage and, believe it or not, they poured new bearings for me! They actually dismantled the engine, scraped out the old bearings, poured in new white metal and rebuilt the engine for me. It only took about two days and I went on my way!'

Rolls was taken aback by the Royce car, and not least by its advanced electrical ignition, which Royce had designed himself. A partnership was struck up and Rolls was contracted as the sole agent to sell Royce cars, renamed as Rolls-Royces. Soon a four-cylinder version was built, and Rolls won the 1906 Tourist Trophy race in the car. As a result, the Rolls-Royce Company was formed and with it the best car in the world was born: the new six-cylinder 40/50hp Ghost model.

Tragically, Rolls was killed in an air crash in 1910, and Royce, who was in his forties when he met Rolls, became ill the following year and was forced to relocate to the South of France. But the exemplary quality of the company's product was unrivalled, and with Royce at the technical helm from his French base and his English home in West Sussex until his death in 1933, the company's products remained at the forefront of both motor car and aero-engine engineering, as arguably they are today.

### HENRY FORD AND THE PIONEERING MODEL T

At the time of the Rolls-Royce Ghost's competition achievements, the international motor industry had grown to such an extent that motoring for the masses had become an accepted possibility. One man was responsible for this – Henry Ford. He was one of America's earliest automobilists and had fought for the rights of the American people to design and build automobiles freely when he started his company in 1903. From the outset Ford was convinced that mass-production methods were the only answer to producing inexpensive automobiles in quantity. He also saw the great importance of keeping the vehicle under-stressed, simple and strong but light. In fact, Ford was virtually obsessed with lightness, but not at the expense of strength, and having cut his production teeth on his Model A in 1903, and the B,C, K and N soon afterwards, Ford prepared for a production line like no other – at Highland Park, Michigan – to build a car like no other: the Model T.

The T was extraordinary, not only because it was successfully built on a moving production line, with its assembly operations timed to the precise moment, but also because it was all things to all men. It was the only car that the American nation truly needed. It was dead reliable, apparently indestructible, an idiot could drive it after a lesson or two, and it could seemingly travel almost anywhere with its high-power, low-revving, 3-litre engine. It was incredible, too, that the T was produced in huge quantities for the time (10,706 in the first full year of production) and yet worked properly right from the outset. There were barely any teething problems.

Henry Ford had achieved with the Model T what Henry Royce had with the Ghost: he'd got it absolutely right first time. Production of the T rose to 18,664 units in its second year of mass production and the figures virtually doubled every year thereafter, culminating in the production of 533,921 cars in 1916. The T came to Britain in 1911 and brought Ford's mass-production methods to the doorsteps of the British motor industry. The following year, William Morris started building cars in Oxford.

Two period drawings from the 1908 Rolls-Royce catalogue, 'The Ideal Car'. They show two 40/50 Ghost tourers motoring in an altogether more refined fashion than their rivals on the road. On its launch in 1907, the Ghost was indisputably 'The Best Car in the World' and the model deservedly remained in production until 1925.

*Above: This was Ford's
first British production
line. It opened on 23rd
October 1911 and in two
years was producing
6000 Model Ts per year.
It closed in 1931 just
as Ford's Dagenham
plant was opening.*

*Right: The Model T
came in many guises,
even as a superb
landaulette. This is 1914
and the Mayoress of
Huddersfield appears to
be at the wheel.*

## THE GENIUS OF WILLIAM MORRIS

William Morris was hardly in a position to mimic Ford's enormous enterprise in London, and was not at all convinced that the big-engined utilitarian machine was right for the British market in any case. Its engine was large, its bodywork tinny (the T wasn't called the Tin Lizzie for nothing), and its road manners were very unrefined. Morris set about building a proper English car, mindful of the Ford's £160 price tag. To do this he bought in ready-made major components and assembled them to a strict budget, producing the 1-litre, four-cylinder Oxford in 1912. Although only a two-seater, it was as English as the T was American, and at £175 it was a joy. The larger Cowley arrived the following year after Morris had visited America to buy the suitable Continental Red Seal engine. After visiting Ford's incredible factory in Michigan, Morris incorporated the first of his methods at Oxford.

William Morris brought mass-production to the British motor industry, and in the nick of time. The First World War denuded the nation of cars, and most were sacrificed in France as they attempted to support the British armed forces, who initially had no mechanised vehicles of their own. The War was to be won with infantry and horsemen, according to the military strategists. Fortunately, the mechanised miracle of the tank appeared in time to stop the tragedy, but not before 10 million troops were dead.

After the First World War, the English, French, Belgian, Italian and German economies were decimated, and America's soon followed suit. Those who had survived the fighting abroad came home to disrupted industry and a shortage of raw materials and facilities. There were few jobs to be had and prices were rising fast. It was a period of great social unrest, and the thought of motoring for the masses was a distant dream. The cars that were available were very expensive, and Britain's domestic products were considerably dated in comparison with America's offerings. Despite heavy import taxes, the Americans sold plenty of thirsty vehicles to Europe immediately after the war, even though petrol was over twice the price that it had been before the fighting began.

The only thing for the motor industry to do was to cut prices viciously, and many firms did not survive the initiative. Ford started the ball rolling and quickly acquired a $50,000,000 debt after the first year in which discounted Ts were sold. The many British makes followed suit and fortunately the market quickly regained its pace. But now manufacturers knew that the key to survival lay in building economical small cars to a low price. The golden era of the Edwardian exotics was over. Now motoring was an industry destined to cater for the masses.

*The ubiquitous 'Bull-Nose' Morris Cowley, here in not-so-rakish two-seater guise. The Cowley and its smaller brother, the Oxford, were the first all-British mass-produced cars, although the Cowley initially used American-manufactured components.*

# Chapter 2

## THE GARAGE

Young and keen or old and blasé, clean and sharp or grubby and blunt, the 'garagist' has always been a charismatic cliché and is one of the great professional manifestations of the 20th century. He didn't exist in Britain before then, but he has more than made up for lost time.

In the early decades of the automotive age the garagist soon became a pillar of the community. Ever the reluctant hero, he gained undeniable status, often operating from the most impressive non-ecclesiastical building in the village, decorated with festoons of tools and clusters of bikes and motors. Small boys would flock there to look, learn and dream while adults spent money there to solve their regular technical crises. The handle had broken on a hoe; the rollers on the mangle were jammed; fuel was needed for the stove; the phonograph wouldn't play; the forks of a bicycle were bent; a motorbike, or even a motor car, needed to be purchased, greased, repaired or sold. The garagist attended to all these things and many more besides, and so became the hub around which the wheel of the locality revolved.

Most garages evolved from established coachbuilders, cycle shops or the iron-mongery and blacksmith trades. For them, becoming a garagist was a natural and obvious transition to make. After all, if there was an automobile in the vicinity it was only a matter of time before its weal-thy owner appeared at the craftsman's gate needing a helping hand. Blacksmiths and ironmongers could mend the broken iron-work, not least springs, axles, chassis and shackles; coachbuilders could attend to the vehicle's body problems; engineers were consulted as to why the works wouldn't perform; and cycle shops possessed the tooling and materials required for maintenance operations. Having witnessed the un-precedented boom of the cycle business during the 1890s, many reasonably predicted that the automobile was going to be the next big thing. And so the garage was born.

*Above: The first garages were direct descendants of old-established trades, frequently the blacksmiths, who were able to work the heavy iron components.*

*Pages 56-57: A proud day for some enthusiastic garagists as a dressy Talbot-Darracq wafts a hint of cosmopolitan Paris about their oily overalls.*

### CYCLE SHOP ORIGINS

According to the author Llyn Morris, the word 'garage' was probably first used in the spring of 1899 by the cycle agent Frank Morris of King's Lynn, who had borrowed the term from France where a garage was a wide section of a French canal constructed so that barges could pass by one another. However, David Burgess-Wise, writing in the *Daily Telegraph* in 1995, claimed that the motoring pioneer Evelyn Ellis christened his specially-built

*A typical pioneer's garage in the early 1900s sported an assortment of motorised transport. This is Webber's of Basingstoke – a company that still thrives today.*

motor house a 'garage' in 1895. Whatever the case, the cycle business was certainly the most common origin of the commercial garage. An astoundingly innovative invention, the cycle provided unheard of speed, practicality and agility, despite the extraordinary need for the rider to balance upon it. Furthermore, the cycle was relatively inexpensive, and with its circus-act appeal and clear transport benefits it caught on very quickly.

Meanwhile, the cycle engineer became the thinking man's blacksmith. He had mechanical sympathies of far greater sophistication than those in the iron crafts and the cycle engineer's spanners, screwdrivers and assembly techniques were state-of-the-art compared with the imprecisions of the smithy's hammer and anvil.

The cycle engineer and shop owner was also typically an entrepreneur, having had the vision to invest in the bizarre cycle soon after it was invented, and therefore possessing a suitably unprejudiced view of the new motor car which was, in his opinion, full of commercial potential.

It was only logical that some cycle manufacturers fitted engines to their modified cycles to make motorcycles before progressing to make automobiles, too. Humber, Lea Francis, Rover, Singer, Sunbeam, Swift, Star and Triumph were all British car manufacturers that started in this way. (Other British car manufacturers weren't involved initially with cycle-building and progressed straight

## THE COST OF A PUNCTURE

Tyre consumption was a big problem before the 1930s; the Edwardian motorist could spend up to £500 a year replacing them. 'Tarmacadam' roads were still rare as late as the 1920s, and one or more punctures per journey could be expected. Tyre-changing was an arduous business, as described in *The Car Illustrated* in 1902: 'Oh! The obstinacy of it! Oh the sore fingers, pushing and shoving to allow the valve to get through into its place! The tricks and artifices we used were many and wonderful ... A new cover [tyre] takes a lot of coaxing.' An early accessory was the 'Stepney Wheel', a spare wheel that could be fixed to the side of the punctured item and serve to get the car home or to a garage.

Below: The superb ex-headquarters of the Michelin tyre company in London's Fulham Road. Perfectly preserved to this day, the building was designed as a corporate advert as much as a pure utility.

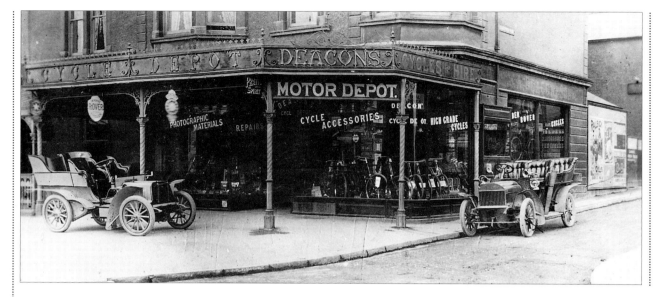

*Above: This telling photograph shows how one high-street shop catered for everything state-of-the-art in 1903. 'Deacons' has photographic, cycle and motor departments advertised on its impressively ornate frontage.*

*Right: The place where British mass-production was founded – William Morris's Longwall Street, Oxford garage pictured in 1912, and clearly advertising Morris's cycle-agent and garagist origins.*

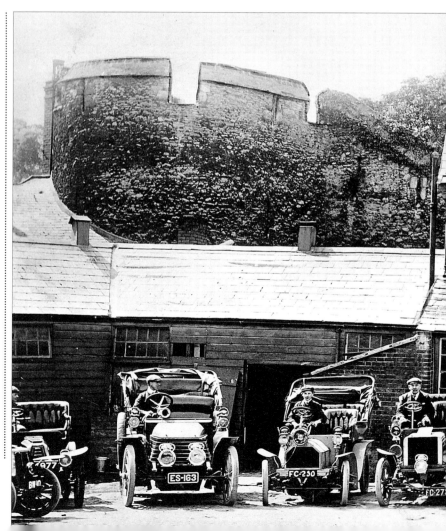

from building motorbikes to cars – Clyno, Jowett and Lagonda among them.) Naturally, the cycle shops followed the trend set by so many cycle manufacturers of selling motorbikes and motorcars from the same premises. Indeed, one such cycle agent, William Morris, later Lord Nuffield, went on to design, manufacture and sell his motor cars from his garage in Oxford before bringing mass-production line techniques to the British industry with his Morris Oxford (see Chapter One).

Although blacksmiths' and ironmongers' premises had been suitable for cycles, they were inappropriate for housing and repairing motor cars, so the creation of the purpose-built garage was inevitable. Cars were tall and took up a lot of space, and for stocking fuels and oils the garage required specialist storage facilities and a convenient location. Soon the mechanic's machine tools and work areas would demand even more space and an electrical supply. According to Llyn Morris, probably

## FROM CYCLES TO CARS — AND BACK

The Peugeot brothers – the first mass-producers of cars in France – are an excellent example of cycle-producer turned motor manufacturer, not least because the Peugeot company still mass-produces cycles and cars. Ironically, now that environmental issues have fuelled interest in cycles again, other motor manufacturers are returning to cycle manufacture, most recently among them Lotus and Aston Martin in Britain.

*Workmen removing signs from a Berkshire village garage during the 1930s. Such commercial decorations were hardly welcome in the picturesque English country village, and legislation eventually prevented the motor trade from adulterating many a fine vista.*

## PETROL PALACES

Until the 1927 Roadside Petrol Pumps Act allowed local councils to license and locate sites, petrol pumps sprang up in all manner of places. The following year, the Petroleum Act allowed councils further power to control the locations of garages that sold petrol and the look of the buildings. These recommendations caused all manner of bizarre retrospective buildings to appear, some looking like Tudor-beamed round houses, others oriental temples. This was the beginning of the specialist garage architecture trend, which boomed in the creative 1950s.

the first purpose-built garage in the country was built by H.W. Egerton and G.N.C. Mann in 1901 at 5 Prince of Wales Road, Norwich. Only a dozen years later, Mann Egerton had sold 3600 cars. Today, Mann Egerton thrives as one of Britain's largest motor car dealerships.

With generally little capital available, the Edwardian garagist established his premises as cheaply as possible. The result was many a blot on the landscape as utilitarian, galvanised-iron buildings sprang up, largely uncontrolled by legislation (law revisions only affected the look of garages in 1928), on land bought cheaply during the agricultural depression. What was more, the garage's services were advertised on garish, large-letter signs emblazoned not only on the premises' walls but also on the roadside, giving all due warning to the hurtling motorist of the services '100 Yards on Left'.

### POOR PETROL AVAILABILITY

The availability of petrol was a major influence in the siting of the garage premises. Fuel was distributed from the main suppliers by rail, and from there to the retailer by his own means. The garage was therefore located near to the railway, and near to the main road or village where the customers were most likely to be found.

Before the arrival of the petrol pump in 1914, obtaining fuel was a laborious business due to a distribution system geared more to the pleasure motoring of the privileged few than to the working motorists of the future. Although there had been marked improvement since the pioneering days, when benzine fuel was purchased by motorists from chemists' shops in bottles, the Edwardian motorist still had to rely on all manner of different fuels made available at either the local garage (if one existed) or a variety of other establishments, ranging from the local hardware store to the village pub. Fuel was bought in 2-gallon tins, with different companies painting their various containers in different colours.

The motorist was left to experiment to find which fuel was most agreeable to his car and style of driving, and strong loyalties developed. The version distributed by Carless, Capel and Leonard was a particular favourite. It was

*Petrol distribution as it used to be. Horse-drawn wagons transported brand fuels (such as Pratt's Motor Spirit) in 2-gallon tins, which were stocked by all manner of retailers from the local pub to the blacksmith and, of course, the garage.*

distributed in round cans, three cans to the crate, and was called petrol – an unpatented name soon to be acquired by all their rivals for similar fuels.

The establishment of petrol pumps was the biggest factor in improving the fuel distribution network and the profitability of selling petrol. But despite the pump's economies of scale, it was not an instant success. It was an expensive machine to buy and fit, requiring a 500-gallon fuel tank to be sunk below it. To operate commercially, it also required a regular delivery from the somewhat irregular petrol tanker.

### THE SPREAD OF THE PUMP

In due time, petrol companies offered services to pay for the installation of tanks and pumps on credit, thereby tying in the garages to their fuel contracts for long periods. Until then garages, post offices, shops and pubs had gradually acquired their own pumps, before the AA gave impetus to the pumping movement by launching their innovative network of drive-in, roadside filling stations in 1919. The first was opened at Aldermaston in Berkshire and that initiative marked the beginning of the age of the petrol station (as distinct from the all-purpose garage).

The supply of petrol to the motorist was something of a nuisance to the garagist. It was a necessary evil to provide it, but the profit margin on its sale, whether by can or, later, pump, was not large – typically a penny per gallon – and a full-time fuel-seller or pump attendant was an inconceivable luxury to those who sold much less than a hundred gallons per day. Furthermore, the sale of fuel badly impinged on the garage's repair work, the garagist having to 'down tools' to attend to the frequent visits of the petrol customer.

This was such a serious problem for the low-staffed garage that it was a wonder any substantial jobs were completed in economic time. Only during the mid-twenties, with the establishment of the multi-brand garage for the burgeoning motoring population, would a pump attendant be viable for many (there were nearly a million motorists in Britain by 1930, almost ten times the figure of a decade before).

By the end of the 1920s, petrol prices were nearly half the 2s per gallon that had been charged in 1922, and it wasn't

*A revolution in fuel distribution took place with the advent of the tanker lorry and the forecourt pump. Fuel would be stored underground in 500-gallon tanks.*

for another ten years or so that prices rose again (from around 1s 1½d in 1936 to 1s 7d in 1938), but that was thanks to the increase in tax on petrol sales, not garage profit. 'The price of petrol may be expected to go up until a satisfactory substitute is found,' wrote two prophetic American motorists Mr and Mrs E.K. Purchase in 1902, having witnessed a 400 per cent rise in the price of petrol in America since 1899 (a trend not mirrored in Great Britain, where fuel prices actually fell over this period). They added: 'It is quite certain that the use of a liquid fuel will still be largely extended in the next few years.'

With small profit margins, strict selling regulations and poor distribution systems (at least before the widespread use of tanker lorries), the relationship between the garagist and the petrol companies was destined to be an uneasy one. But the bond between the garagist and his customer was potentially much stronger – and far more profitable.

*The first pumped fuel station, set up by the AA at Aldermaston in Berkshire. Note the AA man's first-aid kit strapped to his back.*

## HARRY BAGGS REMEMBERS – EARLY PETROL SALES

'My father obtained a licence from the local council in 1912 to store 22 gallons of petrol. Then it used to be delivered in a horse-drawn conveyance which had racks for the petrol cans. It was distributed by a Gloucester firm – Gloucester Motor and Cycle Accessories. You could sell ten cans and then you had to re-order. When I first had a bicycle I used to have to visit customers, to take their petrol orders, deliver the cans and bring back the empties. That was the way petrol was distributed from the garage. Then the kerbside petrol pump appeared in about 1920/21, but soon after that the local council decided that petrol pumps on the pavement were causing an obstruction so they had to be moved.

'My father then had three 500-gallon tanks put into the ground with three Milwaukee suction pumps. One of those, pumping Dominion fuel, was later replaced with the first electric pump in Gloucestershire, but he later abandoned that because it was inaccurate and we went back to the two remaining hand pumps.

'As for choosing from the variety of petrols on offer, it's like your drink at the pub. You have a favourite beer and you have a favourite petrol. Some brands of petrol suit particular cars better than others... It's up to the individual customer, the way they drive, the terrain in which they operate. National Benzole mixture, for example, had a high benzole level and so was an anti-knock fuel, ideal for motorists in hilly countryside because it delayed the ignition speed in the cylinder and prevented "pinking". Cleveland fuel, on the other hand, had a high methanol content and so gave the car a bit more speed.'

Above: A model purpose-built filling station boasting two rival petrol brands and illuminated pump bowls.

Right: Most early motorists had a favourite petrol brand, different petrols suiting different cars and driving styles. At least five brands are offered here at the Kennings garage in Buxton.

## THE AMATEUR BECOMES EXPERT

For the most part, small garagists developed loyal relationships with their customers, even if the qualifications of their staff were no greater than their self-professed levels of mechanical aptitude (and most communities had contenders). Nevertheless, a rich variety of practical skills was born out of military service in the First World War, and these skills were valuable to mechanics, who now had to be able to apply themselves to a wide range of problems on an equally wide variety of cars. For in the days before mass-production and dealer franchises, all manner of different makes and models would be deposited at the garage for repair, and broken parts usually had to be repaired or refabricated on the site. Stockpiles of parts for many models were impractical. Besides, if new parts were required they could take weeks to arrive, not least because long shopping lists of parts often had to be compiled before an economic trip could be made to fetch them.

If pre-First World War cars were driven kindly and serviced regularly, they were largely very reliable between engine overhauls and tyre changes, certainly if they had been built after about 1910. The mechanics of such vehicles were relatively straightforward, and service components were not unduly costly to replace or were easily mended. Although early professional car users, such as doctors or farmers, changed their car every three years or so, it was common for Edwardian and Vintage motorists to keep their vehicles for more than ten years, despite the rapid technological advances. This speaks volumes for the durability of the machines. With the coming of mass-production, the variation of parts fitted between makes was also rationalised considerably, which helped the garages to familiarise themselves with parts and buy them more cheaply and easily. It was only such service economies that tempted many earlier buyers to change up to a newer car.

In addition to the routine service and maintenance work that

### A YOUNG MAN AT THE GARAGE

The earliest motoring memories of Niel Fraser from Southport were of 'the local ironmonger delivering petrol in red cans, transported in a huge wheelbarrow with a strap round his neck' and the 'slatted-side Shell wagons delivering the stock to his shop'. His later memories were of: 'Appy's pub at Highton with its sign outside, reading "Fill up here with Shell and beer." That miraculous pump never ran dry. Even during the Second World War, when we made our visit to Appy there was always a drop of petrol in that pump to get us home.' Like so many young men, Niel taught himself to drive ('The old man simply moved over one day and said "drive"'), and he was to work at the family garage as soon as he left school. It was the late thirties by then. Niel's garage, which had started out as a cycle-makers, stocked the superb Brough Superior cars, a luxury marque which only lasted four years, to 1939. 'I recall at the ripe old age of 17 being sent to Nottingham to collect a six-cylinder supercharged Brough. George Brough, after showing me the various knobs, saw me off with the warning to keep it down to 70.'

*Never mind the fact that it was a French De Dion Bouton, the educated mechanic was an international engine doctor and knew his knocks from his frappés.*

*Service while you wait: a mechanic attends to an AA customer's tourer. Serving petrol was a mixed blessing for the garagist, who could seldom justify the expense of a dedicated pump attendant, and so frequently had to 'down tools' to serve a couple of gallons.*

## IMPROVEMENTS IN SERVICING

By the 1930s, car service intervals had hardly improved. The numerous greasing points on a car had to be attended to every 500 miles, and a major service, including all oils changed, done every 1000 miles or so. Antifreeze did exist, but it didn't have a corrosion inhibitor so it was usual to drain radiators overnight. Batteries were relatively weak and usually had to be charged at the garage and conserved thereafter. It was also usual to turn the car on the starting handle to 'stir' the heavy engine oil before expecting the battery to help. Running-in – or driving with a limited engine speed – was essential when driving a new car, if only to allow the crudely-forged components to 'wear-in' to their new surroundings. A 2000-mile period was commonly recommended, with various oil changes along the way. After the Second World War, nylon and rubber bushes, fluid-filled shock absorbers, factory-warranted replacement parts, and multigrade motor oils reduced service intervals and running-in periods while helping the garage to shorten its job times – all essential advances as the volume of garage work increased dramatically with the popular demand for the motor car. Increased volume also resulted in the need for bigger premises and more costly equipment (see below). The solution lay in the franchise business, as pioneered by Ford. Only then could the capital expenditure be made to pay.

*Opposite: The country garage ideal as portrayed by Mobiloil during the Vintage period.*

was required for the Veteran, Edwardian or Vintage car, decarbonising (the 'decoke') was needed every 10,000 miles or so. Decoking was necessary because carbon deposits would build up around the valves and on the tops of an engine's pistons. These deposits would foul the engine and drastically reduce its efficiency. Decoking an early Edwardian car could be a very involved operation, engines in those days not being constructed in two halves as those in later Vintage cars tended to be. A decoke therefore necessitated lifting the pistons from the main body of the engine. With the advent of the detachable head this process could be avoided. The solution was to take the top off the engine and overhaul the valve gear, cleaning, re-machining or replacing valves as required – a day's work.

Full engine overhauls were also comparatively common, due largely to unsympathetic driving, frost damage, or engines running too low on oil. The quality of metals used in such early motors was not great, and the forgings and bearings employed were vulnerable to punishment.

Unlike in the post-Vintage years, when exchange factory engines were available, at least for some of the mass-produced models, the early garage could afford no such luxury and would have to rebuild all manner of engines on site. Such a system would involve painstaking machining, grinding and boring processes as over-sized pistons were made to fit rebored engine blocks, and white-metal bearings were poured to fit newly ground crankshafts and big ends. Most country garages were not connected to the mains electricity supply until well after the Second World War, and such establishments would have to farm out machining processes that required high-powered electric tooling.

### A WIDE VARIETY OF SKILLS

Rather than getting bogged down in mechanical jargon, suffice it to say that the pre-Second World War garagist had to be able to tackle common problems requiring engine, gearbox and back axle rebuilds, in addition to routine steering, clutch and brake overhauls and servicing. Imagine, for example, the ingenuity and skill required if one of the car's many gear wheels had broken some teeth. Today, a garage would simply fit a new gear,

# How to buy oil!

~ cheaper
~ cleaner
~ quicker

SHELL

MOTOR OIL

In the golden age of motoring, oil was served by Brando-esque attendants with chiselled features and model physiques who posed by oil-pumping machines. From the safety of your natty yellow sports car, it was possible to flirt with the attendant, smiling broadly while pointing a white-gloved forefinger at his jug. Clearly, however, there was no such forecourt fun in the 1960s – at least, Mobil didn't think so.

obtained off the shelf from the parts store or acquired from the manufacturer overnight. Before the Second World War, though, a garage might
well repair the gear by building up metal in the area of the broken tooth,
using gas-welding techniques, before carefully grinding down the new blob
of weld to replicate the tooth that had been broken off. The same levels of
ingenuity were applied to all manner of problems, the garagist rolling new
springs, mending broken drive-shafts, cutting new nuts and bolts, refacing
worn clutches with new leather (later replaced by the Ferodo material) and,
before the First World War, even filling early lighting systems with carbide.

To help himself, the wise garagist dug a working pit, built ramps, taught
himself to weld and acquired an electricity generator. Large country houses,
farms and garages were the most common owners of generators, made by
companies like Drake and Gorham, which produced a noisy 50 watts of
power from their belt-flapping, paraffin or petrol-fuelled devices. Such low
levels of power were sufficient to power tools (via belts running down from
overhead drive gantries) and light rooms, run the petrol pumps and, most
memorably, light the translucent globes on top of them.

'At night,' recalls James Lazenby, whose father's garage was located on
the A40 in Gloucestershire from 1935, 'the only lights visible from the main
road were the globes on top of the petrol pumps. These displayed Shell,
Cleveland Discol and National Benzole.' James' father's garage came with
an inn, and the rent for the lot at that time was £26 per year. Only the
garage had electric lighting, the inn relying on common gas lighting. Most
significant, perhaps, was the fact that the electric Wayne petrol pumps
fitted by Mr Lazenby after he acquired the lease were, according to James,
'the first electric ones within an area of some 10 miles'. Yet three years later
more than 98,000 petrol pumps were operating in Britain, selling between
them a staggering 834 million gallons a year. 'Not many people could afford
or aspired to car ownership,' explains James, 'but those that did needed far
more regular and emergency repairs than those of today. Added to the car
and motorcycle repair pressures were calls to breakdowns of lighting plants
and an increasing demand for attention to farm tractors which were rapidly
supplanting the working shire horses. Another diversity was that of taxi
work, shared mainly with the local blacksmith.'

## TAXI WORK

Taxi work, by either car hire or licensed hackney carriage, was an important
source of revenue for the pre-Second World War garagist, particularly
during the Edwardian and Vintage periods. Harry Baggs is an 87-year-old
garagist still working from his premises in Cheltenham. His father eventually operated six chauffeur-driven hire cars, two of them operating as
hackney carriages. For him hire cars were his main source of income. He
started with a 1911 Cadillac and had two hire cars by the time the First
World War broke out. They were used by local aerodrome customers and
by locals wanting to go shopping, or to the doctor's or the dentist's. 'Shopping

trips were a very important part of the business,' recalls Harry, 'and a great many of the gentry in the town who didn't own a motor car were prepared to hire a car and chauffeur for a week or a fortnight. It continued into the 1920s. There were lots of moneyed people who couldn't drive or didn't have the facilities for a chauffeur and their own car, and they were quite content to pay my father a reasonable sum to hire a car and driver.'

But as cars became cheaper and easier to drive, so the hire-car business died a natural death and the garagist concentrated his energies on maintaining the new volume of cars on the road and recovering crashed cars – which were becoming alarmingly common on the more crowded and ill-disciplined roads of the 1930s.

### THE PERSONAL COST

The workload for the early garagist was enormous, and if money was made the price of success was high. James Lazenby says of his father: 'He was a seven day a week man, starting at half eight and going on until anywhere between ten and midnight. I mean literally he never stopped, going from

*The hire-car business was important to the pre-war garagist. Most people couldn't afford a car, so paying for the occasional use of a chauffeur-driven vehicle made sense. The Australian cricket team were using a fleet of Standards when this picture was taken (date unknown).*

*Above: Accident recovery was a growth business until after the Second World War, and the purpose-built breakdown lorry (or 'wrecker') was a valuable tool, especially if the Morris you were towing had lost both its back wheels...*

one job to the next. I might even say that later on, when I got married, he still hadn't got time. He didn't come to my wedding; he didn't come to my sister's wedding; he didn't even speak to my wife for five to six years after we were married. He just never stopped working.' James Lazenby's story may seem extreme, but it wasn't so untypical. Many a country or village garage was run as a family concern, the son apprenticing in the garage during the war years as staff were drafted to fight abroad, and inheriting the business later on, often sacrificing his own career ambitions in the process.

Wives were obliged to do the books; billing could be haphazard; accounts were often shambolic; the garage floor was invariably disorganised and facilities were behind the times – tooling or machinery was often only bought when legislation or suppliers demanded it. And much as the garagist was a respected member of the community and his garage a meeting-place for so many friends and customers, the country garage dream was often realised only at the expense of the garagist's family life. There was an alternative, at least for the bigger garages, but it was one that many garagists considered unacceptable: to become a Ford dealer.

## GARAGIST OR BUSINESSMAN?

According to James Lazenby, his garagist father probably earned a lot of money but, because there were no accounts, much of what was made was stashed away or never billed for in the first place. James' father stored cash in his bee-hives or buried it, where it devalued enormously before it was recovered, or else just went mouldy. Like many wives of garagists, James' mother was responsible for billing, but because her husband never told her what jobs he'd done, only a portion of it could ever be logged. After James took over the business, his wife was also persuaded to do his book-keeping, and she had to give up a well-paid job at the local RAF station to do so. 'The biggest problem,' considers James, 'is that it wasn't just my father... As soon as I was married I carried on just like my father did, which was terrible for my wife, and I regret it absolutely now because I spoilt some of the best years of her life. I carried on like that until I was 50 years old. So I'm afraid that the one example didn't help the other.'

### THE ROOTS OF THE MODERN GARAGE

Just as Henry Ford had streamlined manufacturing processes in his factories with the introduction of precision-timed mass production techniques, so Ford devised a dealer network which was a model of slick organisation. Those who chose to subscribe to the Ford method were among the modernists of the garage trade. In becoming Ford dealers they lost a great deal of their independence, and many a garagist didn't fancy being told how to run his business. Ford therefore struggled to find dealers initially, but those who did embrace the Ford method often made life much easier for themselves; as the message spread, so did the dealer network, and Ford began to create a nationwide identity that no other manufacturer could boast.

Fundamental to the Ford method was that a Ford garage was a Ford garage exclusively, selling or servicing only Fords in a manner that Ford dictated. To a certain extent the design of early Fords, and certainly the Model T, dictated the need for specialist service in any case, because the Ford was less mechanically conventional than other popular makes. Ford rather arrogantly assigned franchises only to large garages (which could cope with a high volume of business), leaving the smaller independent establishments to sell rival cars, like those from Morris, Austin, Bean and Clyno.

Typically, the independent garagist could purchase a car of any make (and there were, literally, hundreds of makes established by the 1930s) on behalf of a particular customer. He would have it delivered to his garage and then prepare it for sale – he might even teach the customer how to drive the machine as well. The garagist would negotiate a commission from the car manufacturer's supplier and would frequently also take on the responsibility of guaranteeing the car afterwards, usually for a period of 12 months. After-sales service of that type is not just a feature of more modern times – the early garage had its ethical obligations, too.

The Ford garagist didn't have to get involved in complicated purchase neg-otiations for individual cars and was bound by statute to provide standards of sales and service which were of Ford's corporate design. The Ford philosophy was simple: you look after us, and we'll look after you; and although dealers were subjected to punishing stock-purchasing agreements (especially in 1920 when Ford forced dealers to buy cut-price stock in the middle of the Depression, or lose their franchises), by and large the methods worked well.

*Above: The Ford dealer machine was the most effective in the quantity-car business. Below: The era of the salesman had begun when the Argyll factory displayed their cars in this showroom.*

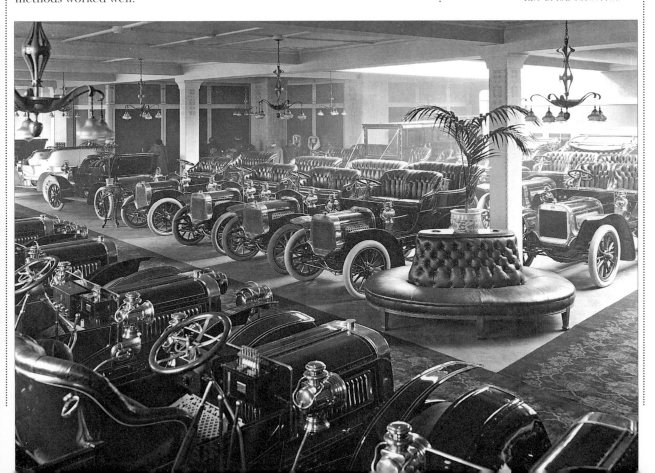

*Top: Even this modest showroom (in York, 1933) promises a good show of salesmanship.*

*Bottom: Dealer franchises in urban areas brought larger premises and many more cars. This is the Austin garage in 1952.*

As the film *SOS* (Service or Slovenliness) produced by Ford in 1935 amusingly illustrates, the company had by then implemented workflow methods, job cards, electronic diagnostic equipment and specialist service bays on the garage floor for carrying out certain specialised jobs – to say nothing of such notions and devices as service-with-a-smile and clean uniforms for all workers. The Ford company continued to lead the way in these working methods for decades to come, and clips from their corporate training films show how concerned they were to employ a very different commercial philosophy from the carryings-on of the rest of the motor trade. Or so they would have had you believe.

### A ROGUISH REPUTATION

Waving the magic wands of fabricating, servicing, repairing and supplying, the garagist turned his valued talents into potent commercial devices, and as the garage became the second home of the oft-broken motor, so the roots were planted for the garagist's roguish reputation. Before the First World War his skulduggery, if it existed, was likely to be confined to charging unpredictable sums to the well-to-do customer for services which the ignorant motorist could neither quantify nor value. Then, with the rapid increase in supply of and demand for affordable transport in the 1930s, so the garagist's sales operation gained pace. Then he was truly able to capitalise on his power to 'give as he taketh away': to supply new vehicles to the starry-eyed grateful as readily as he charged them to keep them on the road. A splendidly effective business premise.

These days, when the modern franchised garage is overseen by a disciplined parent organisation, the motor trade's dubious reputation is generally less deserved, at least in the new car arena, but in days of yore the customer could only be optimistic. The fact remained that both salesman and mechanic were all-powerful when it came to charging you for your motoring. Furthermore, both protagonists worked behind the theatrical façade of the garage – the perfect stage for the foilless plot of making money through motors.

It can be argued that it is a misconception to lump those involved in selling cars together with those who mend and attend them. After all, there is a world of difference between the lizard-eyed Mr Flog-it who sells you the car in the first place, and the benevolent Mr Fix-it who does all he can to mend it... isn't there? In reality, though, from the rise of middle-class motoring in the 1930s and later the promise of cars for the masses after the Second World War, the customer would often have to look deep into the dirt of the garagist's fingernails to tell a Dr Jekyll from a Mr Hyde.

The dishonest reputation of the motor trade is easy to understand and richly deserved. The ethical problem in the sale of new cars is based on the dealer working on commission and having to meet sales targets, and the potential has always existed there for malpractice, even if it is curbed to some extent these days by manufacturers' trading rules. But the source of the secondhand car salesman's profit is, almost by definition, dishonest.

The secondhand car dealer has to buy cars as cheaply as possible, while selling them for as much as possible, having spent as little as possible on them in the meantime. This almost inevitably means that he must tell the seller of the car a different story from that which he tells to the eventual buyer in order to justify the inflated forecourt price. With no manufacturer's 'list' prices to restrict him and lots of potential for fabricating service histories, changing recorded mileages, swopping parts or glossing over facts

## FORD'S EARLY SUCCESS

Ford were highly effective at selling cars in America but less so in England because the Model T was a large-engined car less suitable for the British public. In 1921 – by which time the Model T was a dated machine – over 61 per cent of all new cars sold in America were Ts, thanks to a huge, hard-working dealer network. By employing all manner of dealer stunts and by instigating huge selling demands on contractually trapped dealers, the Ford system inevitably worked, but at a high price to the customer. Pettifer and Turner, writing in 1981, remarked that 'bribes were taken, queues were jumped, fictitious charges added and dealers, while alienating the public, grew extremely wealthy'.

SALESMAN. "It is possible that it may interest you to know that our car was driven up all the flights of steps at the Crystal Palace."
INQUIRING VISITOR. "Well—er—not much. You see, I live in a bungalow."

## FORD AND THE VOLUME PHILOSOPHY

David Guest's family has been selling Fords for 81 years in West Bromwich. 'Ford wrote the rule book in terms of how to control their dealers, so that dealers' energies were focused on Ford's business. That was, and is, necessary because selling Fords has always been a tiny-margin business. Ford realised very early on the importance of good service and parts back-up. They recognised that you cannot hold 10,000 different parts and have 200 cars in stock unless you have a sizable territory.'

*The motor trade gave rise to some imposing purpose-built architecture. From the beginning, the garage was often the biggest non-ecclesiastical building in the neighbourhood. This is Ford's palatial Dagenham Motors, London, pictured in 1931.*

that don't support the car's 'new' value, the honest second-hand car dealer must resist the most overwhelming of temptations.

Nowadays, The Trade is a lot more ethical than it used to be, if only because it is easier to be. To-day, cars are so much more reliable than in the past that the risks of buying a 'dodgy' example from a dealer are far smaller than they were even 20 years ago. However, the same risks do still exist, but can be disguised under ever more sophisticated cloaks of respectability. As recently as September 1995 the *Independent on Sunday* reported that a North of England dealer operating 18 franchises was being prosecuted for selling 'clocked' cars (the mileage readings on them were not true records of the actual miles covered). The company chairman had to face 141 charges.

'In the old days,' explains ex-motor dealer Jim Oliver, 'cars used to wear out after about 30,000 miles. They certainly needed a re-bore after that mileage and, without good anti-freeze, car radiators and blocks would frequently crack. So there were many more bad cars around. We didn't like selling duff cars, but cars weren't so strong. We gave our cars a guarantee, but we perhaps used to have to resort to second-hand parts to repair them, because there wasn't much profit to be made.'

Jim also recalls that there were very few dealers selling used cars before the Second World War because cars were costly and credit was hard to get, so it was uneconomical to hold stock. The post-war dealer boom – and the birth of the cash-rich spiv – came about because cars were in great demand and anything, war-worn or not, would sell. 'Raymond Way was a great character – one of the old school of car dealers based in Kilburn. He started in about 1933 and his evening paper adverts used to read "Nothing over £15". He used to say, "Don't come to my showroom expecting carpets on the floor and aspidistras in the showroom. We can't afford that; our cars are too cheap." I met him in 1946, a year after I started up in Forest Hill. He came into my yard – I had about eight cars, all around 1935 models – and he said, "All good runners boy?" I said, "Yes, Mr Way," and he bought the lot, sticking £1 on each because he hadn't the time or the drivers to pick them up.'

While straightforward traders like Raymond Way and Jim Oliver did exist, it was the post-war rise of the spiv that gave the used-car trade its dreadful reputation. All manner of methods would be employed to

keep a car running long enough for it to leave the garage forecourt under its own power. Temporary mechanical 'repairs' involved the use of myriad materials, from sawdust to cement, eggs to porridge and mustard, while structural nightmares came in the form of 2 by 4 inch wooden beams as chassis rails and plaster-of-Paris as body filler, and these habits lasted beyond the austerity years (see Chapter Four). Through the Warren Street trader era in London during the fifties and sixties, when dealers would park their stock in the streets looking for a fast cash deal, to the modern dealers offering finance, hire purchase and complicated guarantees, the nature of the motor-trader beast remains seductively dangerous. In fact, for the experienced, dealing with The Trade has long since become something of a sport.

G.R.N. Minchin recalled in 1950 how the man who was to become the fastest on earth, Malcolm Campbell, was conned, in a manner of speaking, by Charles Lane, 'a well-known dealer in racing cars... in the Euston Road'. The transaction took place around 1914 when Campbell bought a racing Grégoire car from Lane. Campbell was apparently a hard buyer, usually offering around half the asking price, and eventually beat Lane down sufficiently to buy the car. It was only subsequently that Campbell discovered that both spare wheels, set into the running boards on either side of the car, carried badly holed tyres, the damage only being apparent when the wheels were turned in their housings.

*Land speed record-breaker Malcolm Campbell specialised in the sale and service of Bugatti cars.*

In 1954 the writer John Marshall referred to a visit to a London motor dealer as 'a morning of stark horror dealing with the sharp-eyed and ever glibber-tongued ferrets of The Trade'. Marshall, a keen motorist, professed to having been 'the proud possessor of an impressive and fabulously costly range of motor cars'... as a window shopper. He wrote: 'You may stick your nose, like a Bisto kid, against the shining window of a West End showroom and dream your magical dreams; but you will get no further unless you possess a great deal more cheek than most of us and will not quail before the immense superiority of the West End motor salesman so that you will insist upon sitting inside his palatial wares.'

The dark, enticing powers of the motor dealer have barely changed. Like some fallen angel, the dealer struts his seductive fine-cut stuff behind a wall of glass that separates his decorated world from the dirty chaos of the street outside. Proud and protected in his trading castle, he is often a vampire who will suck the most reluctant automotive vanities from anyone who dares to enter.

And so many would, and so many will again.

# Chapter 3

## FREEDOM OF THE ROAD

'The Freedom of the Open Road – what a glorious prospect is bound up in that simple phrase and all that it means to the lover of adventure!' So expounds an enthusiastic Edward J. Burrow in his introduction to Alison D. Murray's informative 1920s pocket-book *Seeing Britain from an Austin*. Quite how different Britain seemed from an Austin than it did when seen from, say, a Morris, let alone an Hispano-Suiza, is not made clear, but what does come across awfully well in Murray's (Austin-commissioned) booklet is that touring in an Austin at the time was terribly jolly and frightfully middle-class. Burrow continues: 'The Austin brings the whole of the country within easy reach of one's door, and laughs at the hills and valleys that lie between us and our once-distant friends. A 25-mile run after tea, a round of golf, or a little tennis, or a quiet talk and home again before dark is an easy venture in the long summer evenings...'

Just what sort of Austin Mr Burrow is referring to here is hard to imagine. Take it from me, any twenties Austin was not a fast car and 'laughing at hills' must have been a nervous reaction at the prospect of them rather than one of powerful confidence. But Burrow's enthusiasm doesn't let up, desperate as he is to get his Austineering message across: 'In anticipation, one thrills with the expectation,' he continues. 'I envy you the

*Pages 82-85: A Morris two-seat tourer and lady friends exploring the British Isles. It sums up the ideal that was the Freedom of the Road.*

*Below: Family motoring outings were synonymous with picnicking. Here a Morris, a Vauxhall and their motorists take a rest.*

delightful sensation you will experience when, the last strap having been adjusted on the luggage grid, and a final look at the map, the starter rushes the engine into life, the friends standing at the door of the old home wave a cheery goodbye, and the Austin moves out through the gateway into the venture land of castles and mountains and placid flowing rivers, lakes, waterfalls, swelling moorlands...'

Ever seen a swelling moorland? Only from an Austin.

But that's how it was. Wasn't it? That's what going off in the car was like in the 1920s, if you were wealthy enough to own one. As I've discussed before, prior to the 1920s motoring was only for the seriously rich, and the pastime usually came with all manner of complications, from chauffeurs and punctures to festoons of cumbersome fashions and weatherproofing appendages. Michael Sedgwick wrote in *Autocar*: 'When we contemplate our Edwardian motorist, struggling with his 29-piece tool kit, and dressing his clutch hopefully with collan oil, we must also remember the compensations. He did not know what a traffic jam was. There was no compulsory insurance, no driving test, and no Highway Code. The Treasury Rating road fund tax had yet to be invented. The highest annual tax levied in 1913 was 21 guineas, for which one could license 15 litres of Opel.' But while the pioneer and Edwardian motorists experienced the first freedom of the open road, true motoring freedom came with owner-driving, reliability, better roads, the stronger pneumatic tyre, widespread and regular fuel distribution, improved comfort and ease of driving, self-starters, no relentless speed-trapping, no serious anti-motorist lobby and, crucially in view of what was to come, no traffic.

*Only in England. Ladies take tea, with their friendly fabric-bodied Standard Teignmouth loyally in attendance.*

This was a combination of factors which only the 1920s motorist experienced in the purest sense. The 1920s was the Vintage era, and the Vintage car has had a starry-eyed following ever since.

## THE GOLDEN VINTAGE AGE

After a slow economic start, the Vintage period saw the introduction of the low-pressure tyre; widely-distributed leaded fuel (which did so much to reduce engine 'pinking' and engine wear); common fitment of four-wheel brakes; improved and standard body constructions, sometimes using fabric-covered frames (of the Weymann type), all-steel pressings (manufactured by Budd) and even unitary chassis-body construction techniques (pioneered by Lancia); and the popular adoption of lighter aluminium pistons in new engine designs that incorporated overhead valves and camshafts. Most

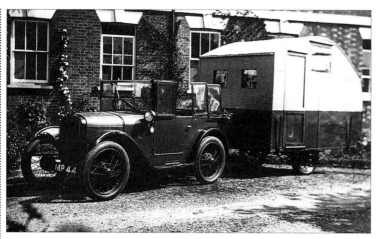

*A 1926 Austin 7 and a diminutive caravan promise many a weekend adventure.*

significantly, though, the Vintage era saw the birth and rapidly growing popularity of the affordable and diminutive 'baby' car as well as the rakish and rousing 'sports' car, in the form of two-seater roadsters and four-seater, low-chassis tourers.

While baby cars allowed a new freedom of the road for many, sports cars gave something more decadent to a privileged few. The sports car owner could not only indulge in the new motorsport events of the era, but he could also court the opposite sex with a new and highly seductive flair.

The baby car was epitomised by the Austin 7 and the Trojan, both launched at the 1922 Olympia Motor Show. These models differed from previous small cars (many of which were crude and lethal evolutions of the bicycle called 'cyclecars') in that they incorporated big car features in baby car design. Both were strong, commodious (four seats), economical (45mpg), simple to

## PETER FALCONER REMEMBERS – CARS AND COURTSHIP

'A friend of mine, John, was forbidden by his mother to use the Humber which was the pride of their lives. She used to check the odometer every night to make sure the car hadn't been used. But John discovered that he could go and see his girlfriend in Cirencester by driving forwards all the way there and backwards all the way back, stopping to top-up the fuel tank. That way, when mother checked the speedometer, it showed exactly the same mileage in the morning as it had the night before.

'You had a sports car primarily to pull the girls. It really started with MGs and the Gordon England Austins, because the people who owned Bentleys and the like were rather older. A number of friends of mine bought sports cars, not for motorsport activities but purely for courting. When you'd bought your MG but you didn't get the girl you'd hoped for, then you went in for motorsport – trials – instead.

'In Cheltenham it was the girls at Cavendish House, a hostel somewhere near the Everyman Theatre. You often used to see 20 or 30 sports cars outside, possibly more, with young men in them, looking hopeful. And in Bristol, where I went to architectural school, there was a great store opposite where there were many pretty girls, and we used to watch the queue of MGs forming from about 5 o'clock in the evening to take the beauties home the moment they'd changed. Occasionally you'd see a more exciting car, like a Triumph Dolomite.

'Then there were the station-wagons. There was hardly a garage in Cheltenham that hadn't got its own station-wagon and they were in great demand every night from the motor salesmen who were a lively bunch of young men! Not only could they "pull the birds" but they could enjoy their company too, usually in the woods around Cheltenham.'

drive and reliably slow (38mph was pushing it for the Trojan). Furthermore, both of them sported four-cylinder engines, instead of the usual vee-twin and flat-twin cylinder affairs of their utilitarian predecessors, and the Austin even had four-wheel brakes. At £165 (£225 initially) for the sprightly Austin and £175 for the stolid, solid-tyred Trojan (as advertised in the *Church Times*), these two models gave big momentum to the mass-motoring drive.

By the end of the decade many other British makes would be competing for buyers in the baby class with cars like the Singer Junior, the Triumph Super Seven and the Clyno Nine. This culminated in Morris's late arrival in 1928 – the Minor – with prices starting from £125. The baby car concept was a hit right from the start, and car designers have never looked back.

The sports car was a truly spectacular invention. Before 1919 (the official start of the Vintage period), sports cars were either highly expensive seldom-seen foreign exotics, built by companies like Hispano-Suiza in France, Mercedes in Germany, Mercer in the US or Métallurgique in Belgium, or hot-rods, constructed either by factories as limited edition racers (like Napier's Hutton in 1908) or by fearless amateurs using aero-engines and redundant big-banger power plants in nondescript chassis. Truly roadable, refined sports cars, however, designed for production and sale in quantity, were a principally British invention from the Vintage age.

*Above: 'I can't come out yet, dear; I'm washing the baby.'*

*Below: Morris's answer to the baby car boom – the Minor, here in handsome saloon guise.*

*The pretty MG Midget was the archetypal budget sports car and the perfect mount for the eligible young man trying his luck. It's 1952, and quite how these Edinburgh policemen can justify patrolling in a Midget is not altogether clear.*

They came in the form of Alvis 12/50s and Aston Martin 1¹/2s; Bentley 3-litres and Vauxhall 30/98s; MGs and HEs; Rileys and Sunbeams; Lagondas and Talbots, GNs and later Frazer Nashes. Like the sensational Italian Alfa Romeos of the later 1920s and 1930s, the finest sports cars were always expensive, but with the burgeoning of amateur motorsport in this country, spearheaded by the Brooklands fashionable society scene at the weekends, even the humble Austins and Morrises received the sports-car treatment. Tweaked engines, brassy fish-tail side exhausts, modified drivetrains and diminutive 'aero' windscreens were all part of the sporty identikit. As the motoring veteran and good ol' Brooklands boy Dudley Gahagan once said to me: 'And believe you me, when you're doing 100mph in an Austin 7 up on the Brooklands banking – then you're really getting on with the washing.'

One of the most vigorous initiatives in establishing a wider market for the automobile took place in the early twenties when Henry Ford (soon followed by William Morris) instigated a wave of new car-price slashing. Apart from forcing many other makes out of business, their actions gave a new momentum to a national car market which was still recovering from the twenties slump. Morris model prices, for example, fell by over half in the two years from 1920. Before the price slashing a professional man, earning perhaps £320 per year, could buy a new common 12hp car for about the same sum. Around £100 more would have bought a 'closed' saloon

*Arguably the finest sports car Britain made before the war, and this country's only equivalent to Italy's 1750 Alfa Romeo – the beautifully proportioned and extraordinarily quick 1934 Riley MPH. Tragically, fewer than 20 were built.*

*Above: A particularly rakish rendition of an Armstrong-Siddeley with delusions of continental grandeur. But what better way to tour than in the back of a big-engined laudaulette?*

*Left: On their way to Olympia. A charming period advert, implying an adventure in store for all the family.*

car. But following the price slashing, and the inevitably cheaper production methods that came with it, less expensive cars boasted better specifications. Self-starters and four-wheel brakes became the norm on the £200 car by the mid-twenties, and barely five years later, in sympathy with the progressive lowering of the cost of motoring, the Ford 8 was launched as Britain's first £100 car.

The tumbling prices go some way towards explaining why there were twice as many cars on the road by the end of the 1930s as there were at the beginning, and why a certain freedom of the road was lost as the Vintage era drew to an end.

## THIRTIES MATERIALISM

So many more cars on Britain's roads during the thirties served four major blows to the freedom of the road ideal: firstly, not only was there a real chance of meeting various other cars on the roads as you motored, but you might conceivably encounter the new 'traffic jam' phenomenon, especially if you motored on a Sunday in coastal districts. Secondly, more cars meant more legislation to control their drivers. Thirdly, more motoring brought with it many more revenue opportunities for the government, so the motorist was taxed more heavily. And lastly, the sort of people buying the new mass-produced cars were far removed from the savoury, dignified, proper vintage types who motored in the twenties, let alone the aristocrats of the Edwardian and pioneer years. In the eyes of the old school, the new middle-class thirties motorist had ideas above his station, and very little taste, too.

The new thirties motorists were the yuppies of their generation – people who wanted a new baby mass-produced car at almost any cost. This was motoring materialism of a type that hasn't been seen before or since. Forget the eighties-style Thatcherite who acquired the new BMW as soon as his credit-line could stand the strain; his or her 1930s equivalent had far more warped materialistic tendencies. Spending as much on a new car as one would on a house was not uncommon in the thirties, and that despite the fact that any new car could devalue by more than 50 per cent a year.

Such monumental motoring decadence is indisputably borne out by the statistics at the time, and I quote from Graham Robson's book *Motoring in the Thirties*. He refers to a survey carried out in 1938, 'when conditions were as favourable as at any other time in the decade'. Robson states, '...the average British family income was of the order of £450 a year and that

### TRAFFIC JAMS

Traffic jams in the thirties were a genuine problem. Although they tended to be confined to main roads, such roads were often the only practical means by which to travel any distance. 'If you were going north on the Great North Road,' recalls Peter Falconer, 'Doncaster was a black spot – you could really queue any day for a long time there, going through the middle of the town. But the worst traffic jams were on Sunday, say from Weston-super-Mare coming back to Bristol, where it could take you four hours to do the 20 miles. There were motor coaches – hundreds of them – all moving slowly so the traffic really couldn't sort itself out. There were very few by-passes in those days and even the single-lane Exeter by-pass suffered from the most enormous jams. On a Saturday it was always a triumph to get around Exeter in under two hours.' Gilbert Everett of Rochester in Kent recalls: 'During the thirties there used to be an enormous volume of traffic on its way to London returning from the south-east seaside resorts on summer weekends. There were coaches, charabancs and cars of all kinds growling their way up Wrotham Hill, with their noisy gearboxes and exhausts; huge motorcycle combinations loaded with wives and kids, thumping full bore. And this would go on until late at night.'

*Opposite: More nuclear-family fun courtesy of the Austin 7. Father's briefcase might seem a mite out of place on the cliff-face, but the point had to be made that the Austin was a car for all occasions.*

*Right: Dad plays the fool while his daughters look embarrassed. A superb happy family photo complete with stately Austro-Daimler, circa 1925.*

*Below: Seaside traffic became intolerable during the thirties as the weekend coastline ritual gained popularity.*

middle-class families might be earning between £550 and £600 a year.' Robson goes on to make the highly significant point that the average industrial wage was just £3 per week (£156 per year) and that as many as 22 million – out of a total working population of under 25 million – earned less than £5 a week (£260 per year).

Bearing in mind these income levels across the population, and the fact that income tax was set at just 14 per cent at that time, it is a sobering thought to consider that Britain's cheapest saloon in 1938 (a new Ford 8) cost £117.10s. That was the equivalent of £3150 in 1995 money and, incredibly, it was as much as an average industrial worker would earn in a year. A civilised, unextravagant family saloon, such as a Triumph Gloria, cost around £285 at the time (£7675 in 1995 money) – more than a whole year's family income for those 22 million people Robson refers to. Incidentally, £2675 (£72,037 in 1995) would have bought you the most expensive car of all on the British market, a Rolls-Royce. That says plenty about how exclusively rich the wealthy were in Britain before the Second World War, even if nowadays a sum around nine times that amount, in real terms, would be needed to buy today's most expensive car – the McLaren F1.

If the proportion of people's incomes being spent then on new cars isn't shocking enough, consider too that the price of an average semi-detached house in Britain during 1938 was between £400 and £500. That, in automotive terms, represented middle-market motoring: Alvis or Armstrong-Siddeley money. Houses, then, were a positive snip compared to cars. What is more, houses were an investment while cars most certainly were not.

The depreciation issue makes the thirties' car boom even more astonishing. According to advertisements placed in *The Autocar* in 1936, a two-year-old Hudson Terraplane saloon, which cost £300 new, could be bought in 'perfect' condition for just £75, while a model a year older was advertised for no more than £39.10s. And these are dealers' asking prices, of course, so, realistically, deals would have been done for substantially lower figures. Even an 'as new' Austin 7 would depreciate by half in its first year, while serious vintage machinery, like the gorgeous 1928 Alvis 12/50 duck's back, advertised in *The Autocar* in 1936, could be bought for £50.

More basic vintage machinery could be had for only a week's wages. As Anthony Wood, from Selsey in West Sussex, recalls: 'Before the Second War you could buy a car of sorts for a couple of pounds. And you could get a good car, one perhaps only three or four years old, for £10. And you could run them on a shoestring.'

*Another splendid period photo shows a newly mobile family proudly posing with their Austin 7.*

## TYPICAL RUNNING COSTS

In 1928 the *Auto Motor Journal* tested the new Rover 10/25 to assess its manufacturer's economy claims and reported: 'A "Nippy Ten", with four-seater fabric saloon body, which was sent out with four occupants and was driven by two ladies starting out to see how far the car could run on a £5 note, has proven the convention of its designers that the new model stands pre-eminent as a vehicle of comfortable and economical motoring. The car ran through England from north to south and from east to west, covering 2147 miles under RAC observation before the £5 note had been expounded.' At 1.58 pennies per mile, that was cheap motoring; but the annual running costs of the little family Rover over 10,000 miles still worked out at £65.15s.6d.

| Cost of running a 1928 Rover 10/25 over 10,000 miles in one year | |
|---|---|
| Oil at 1000mpg (10 gallons) | £02.19.02 |
| Petrol at 38mpg (263 gallons) | £15.06.10 |
| Annual tax | £10.00.00 |
| Driving licence | £00.05.00 |
| Garage at 5s per week for 52 weeks | £13.00.00 |
| Decarbonising (twice) | £03.10.00 |
| Grease (also oil for axle and gearbox) | £00.15.00 |
| Allow for insurance and incidentals | £19.19.06 |
| TOTAL | £65.15.06 |

The absurdly astute, and those with more than shoestrings to run their cars on, could even have bought Woolf Barnato's 1930 Bentley 'Blue Train' Speed Six for £345 in October 1936 (the equivalent today, index-linked, of £9300) according to an advertisement placed in *The Autocar* at the time. But realistically, who at that time was to know that the very same car would sell for £240,000 at a Sotheby's auction in 1984 and be worth perhaps three times that today?

In fairness, the extraordinary need to buy a new car was not only a status issue but was also born out of the need for reliable transport by the professional classes. The reliability factor was an important one in the thirties because the new-era motorist was less likely to use his or her car purely for pleasure and therefore demanded greater reliability from it as a business tool. Furthermore, as the car was no longer purely a luxury, so its driver was less likely to be an enthusiastic amateur mechanic.

Like their Vintage predecessors, most mass-produced thirties' cars needed major work after 30,000 miles, and a new car therefore offered a greater degree of carefree motoring. In comparison, the lovely older Vintage machinery that was available so cheaply at the time would have seemed tired, impractical and, of course, extremely unfashionable.

While those fortunate enough to have been Vintage motorists might well identify those years as the golden years of freedom of the road, those new to motoring in the thirties championed their decade as the best of the century. For despite the increase in traffic, taxes and legislation, the loss of Vintage character and quality from cars, and early industrial unrest, the thirties produced many of the most technically and aesthetically beautiful cars of all time.

In the words of Flower and Wynn Jones: 'The proposition that no decent car was built after 31st December 1930 when Vintage machines are considered abruptly to have ended... is all the more curious since this was the precise moment when the motor car blossomed in a flowering which it had never attained before, and in many ways never matched since.' But Flower and Wynn Jones speak of the 'aristocrats' of motoring: Hispano-Suizas, Isotta Fraschinis, Duesenbergs, Packards, Bugattis and Talbot-Lagos. Such exotica was often foreign and hugely expensive, and many were extinct, if not by the end of the decade, then quite soon after the end of the Second World War. Mass-produced 8 and 10hp cars, around half of which on British roads in the thirties were accounted for by Austin and Morris, were

far less remarkable technically and in their construction; on the other hand, they did provide unprecedented quality motoring for hundreds of thousands of keen motorists. Freedom of the road is therefore relative. Just as today's 17-year-old clutches his driving test pass-certificate with joy at the promise of owning his or her first car, so has every new driver been excited at the prospect of the new freedom ahead. Never mind that mother won't sleep at night, never mind having to borrow the car purchase money, never mind the traffic, pollution, the impossibilities of insurance, garaging, servicing and repairs, a car is still a ticket to status and escape. And so it has always been.

## A NEW FREEDOM FOR WOMEN

While pioneers like Alfred C. Harmsworth were among the first to enjoy the spirit of motoring, justifying its expense primarily on the grounds of health – 'I believe that the brain, nerves and blood are stimulated by rapid transit through the air as by no other means' – women were also to benefit greatly from the true freedom the motor car provided. Until the family car arrived, even the wealthiest of women were relatively housebound, and visiting friends or shopping required considerable planning and oat-bags of horse-drawn hassle. With the arrival of the motor car, whether driven by the chauffeur or the proud lady motorist herself, the delights of daytime duties could be indulged with a new abandon.

### HEALTH, FREEDOM AND THE PIONEER

As early as 1902 the great motoring pioneer and Mercedes 40 driver Alfred C. Harmsworth wrote: 'Even now there are people who have not yet lived – to whom the charms of speed that is always above the legal 12mph are unknown. People are only beginning to learn how much there is of England, of which they know nothing. Then for convenience: working all day at some pressure in London, taking a considerable railway journey followed by half-an-hour in a horse-drawn carriage, I formerly arrived home too tired to exercise. Now I drive the whole distance by road in such time as I will not mention for the benefit of the police, and am able to walk or play tennis.' That same year *The Autocar* reported that one of its staff members counted 23 cars within a space of three-quarters of an hour in London's West End, which implies that Harmsworth was not alone in his commute. In 1995, incidentally, 2,600,000 cars were in use in Greater London, fuelled by 2100 petrol filling stations which sold, every day, enough fuel between them to emit over a ton of lead and over 1.5 tons of carbon monoxide into London's atmosphere. Harmsworth, who claimed to motor 'primarily for the health my household and I derive from it', would surely be appalled.

*Above: Freedom of the road in Westminster? Not for this Humber Snipe it seems!*

*Below: Two ladies and a Peugeot have completed the exclusive and arduous Monte Carlo Rally.*

It was from the era of the pioneer lady motorist that the calling card was brought to eminence. The habit of the time was for ladies to take to the roads in the morning and call on their friends throughout the day, invariably unannounced. Should the friend not wish to be disturbed, the door was not answered (or the butler would say she was out), and so a calling card was left, just to show that a visit had been made. The motor car gave madam some independence at last: motoring required only one essential companion – the chauffeur – and her relationship with (usually) him, if suitably intimate, allowed her some of the privacy and freedom her husband enjoyed every day in business.

Before 1910 and the advent of the light car (smaller, lighter and less powerful models than the common tourer) women often found motoring difficult. Apart from the problems involved with breaking down or tyre-changing, cars were often very heavy to drive and many women were simply not strong enough to enjoy the experience. Just swinging the starting handle on a cold morning was enough to put most of them off. Later, with the advent of the self-starter and numerous other practical motoring conveniences, ladies took to the wheel in tangible numbers – and so they became more directly tormented and ridiculed by the male motoring establishment.

Some men were wiser to the future than others. W.H Berry wrote in 1914: 'We cannot claim that all women are unsuited to be drivers, forsooth, because some are inclined

to be wobbly on the road. For weal or woe we must make up our minds that the lady driver will be seen on the roads in increasing number.'

Perhaps more serious than the battle of the sexes on the roads was the assumption, at any time before the Second World War, that a woman on the road at night could only be a prostitute. Recalling motoring experiences in the thirties, Tom Swallow from Ross-on-Wye in Herefordshire notes: 'It was assumed that if a female was travelling after dark then she was on the game. My wife and I were actually turned away from a transport café where we went for a cup of tea on the Coventry Road one night. We'd been to Dagenham to pick up a new truck, but they wouldn't serve us.'

True freedom of the road for women, then, may be considered to belong to a different era than that for men. With prejudice the most restricting factor, it took the enrolment of women to drive transport during the Second World War to change society's perspective on the women behind the wheel. During the war women were relied upon to drive all manner of vehicles, from heavy trucks to ambulances and local delivery vehicles. And so able were they at the new transport tasks that when the men returned to reclaim their driving jobs after the war, in many cases women were more than ably filling them. Women bus drivers are nothing new, after all.

*Extraordinary car, extraordinary picture: girls having fun in a unique Morris Cowley complete with polished wooden torpedo body and twin spare wheels.*

## FREEDOM FOR THE MASSES

'In about 1936, when I was four years old,' explains Joan Ruston from the Midlands, 'my father had a win on the pools. He won £150, and he knew exactly what he wanted to do with the money. My mother begged him to put a deposit on a house, which at that time would have cost about £400 complete, but he wasn't going to put his money into bricks and mortar: he went out and bought a Ford. I still remember the registration number – AOB 677 – and it transformed our lives because we could go out into the countryside, albeit only on a Sunday.'

Such passionate memories of acquiring a car in the thirties do a lot to explain just how much freedom motoring represented to ordinary people at the time. Rod MacKay, recalling memories as a small boy growing up in Scotland in the thirties, reminisces: 'My father's car introduced me to places

### THIS FREEDOM, ACCORDING TO JOWETT

'For 1000 years we Englishmen have fought for our freedom. Our home is our castle; the highway winds unbarred. Every river is musical with memories; every green field, every beacon hill, is rich with the dust of those who fought for This Freedom. Have you spied the purple iris blossoming along the river bank? Have you glimpsed a bit of heaven whilst picnicking by the scented pinewood? The wind's on the heath, brother; the highway is calling; there's laughter and deep breath and zestful life over there on the hills. Freedom is waiting you at the bang of your front door.' Thus read Benjamin and Willy Jowett's advert for their early-twenties Jowett cars. 'I love to think of you two behind – my master at the wheel, my mistress by his side,' proclaimed in full poetic vein the unashamedly surreal advertisement for the Jowett 7. 'You two shall ride forever thus, and before the shadow lengthens and the violet deepens on the hill you shall experience a new understanding of joy.'

## THE GREAT BRITISH PICNIC

The great British picnic was all-of-a-fashion for the pre-Second World War family motorist, and weekend exeats to grassy banks and byways were very common. Not only would the car take the family to their picnic place but, judging by the numerous period photographs of such occasions, it also seemed to attend, parked like a patriarch somewhere in the nearby background. Rod MacKay recalls his Scottish childhood:

'The picnic was the focus of recreational rambles in the car. They went on right through the summer – a real ritual. It would begin with the preparation of the hamper. That was a big basket that used to sit on the luggage rack at the back of the car. My mother would prepare this on a Saturday evening and then, on the Sunday mid-forenoon, we'd all sally forth in the car with a roadside audience waving to us as we passed. I think our favourite spot was the banks of Loch Ness. We'd spread the tartan rug, get out the strawberries and tomatoes and the sandwiches, together with the Primus stove for the tea. And then there was always lemonade to follow. The only eternal snag was the carnivorous Scottish midgey...' And the atrocious weather.

that I would never have seen otherwise. At that age, if it hadn't been for the car, the boundaries of my entire life would simply have been the outskirts of my little village, but the car introduced me to Dingwall, Inverness, Culloden Moor, Fort George, Fort William, Fort Augustus, Golspie, Rogart, Lairg and so many other wonderful places.

'And the car also showed me something which, although I didn't really appreciate it at the time, has meant much more to me later: sometimes on those desolate tracks of Sutherlandshire among the bogs and peat and heather, I would see from the car small clusters of hillside cottages with no roofs or doors or windows. My father briefly explained to me that the occupants had been got rid of by soldiers a couple of hundred years before. Only now I know of the ubiquitous Highland Clearances, initiated by the Duke of Sutherland on behalf of the Hanoverian kings.'

For children, cars were great fun to ride in, even if their place was invariably in the back and often in the notorious dickey seat – that fold-out arrangement that would appear like a swing-bin from the boot of the car. 'The best bit,' recalls Peter Falconer from Minchinhampton in Gloucestershire, 'was watching the speedometer. I remember so well going down to Bath when we got up to 40mph for the first time. My sister and I were cheering our heads off!'

'It was the children's favourite seat,' remembers C.W. Pearsall from Abingdon in Oxfordshire, 'completely separated from our parents where we could sing pop songs at the tops of our voices.' But Elizabeth Vowles from Whaddon in Gloucestershire wasn't quite so enthusiastic about the experience: 'Being always the youngest of any adult party, I had a fair experience of riding in the dickey. And pretty miserable it was: a hard seat and cold wind, nothing to see but the back of the car's hood in front and isolation if there was no companion.'

According to correspondent Roy Shannon from Reading in Berkshire, Sir Marcus Cheke wrote in his book *The Licking* about his memories of riding as a child with his dog, Bumble, in his mother's new Edwardian Stellite. 'When we had passed Old Sarum I looked behind at the dickie and suddenly discovered that Bumble was lost. It was a dreadful moment. My mother turned the car and we began driving back the way we had come in silence, our hearts filled with anxiety. Just as we were re-entering the first suburbs of Salisbury we met the prodigal. He was padding along the road with an expression of determination in the face of his difficulties, his tongue lolling out of his mouth.'

Anthony Wood was better off in the back of his father's Austin 12-4: 'We had our own windscreen and two side-screens and a travel rug and an apron that used to go over our knees. This had a scissor-type adjuster so we could pull it towards us, rake the screen over and then we felt like we were doing 100mph in the back. Ma and Pa in the front had a bolt-upright screen, though, so they could only ever be doing a sedate 40.'

Perhaps the most exciting motoring prospect for the family during the twenties and thirties was the rapidly growing pastime of camping and caravanning. Peter Falconer: 'When I first went down to Somerset on holidays, we used to go to East Pennard. That was in the early twenties and we went by train, which was a real saga. We had to take a taxi to Worcester station. That was an adventure in itself, because like so many cars at the time, it wouldn't go uphill without using reverse gear. It used to re-verse up Culver Hill from Amberley as a matter of course. Having survived the taxi we then had to go to Stonehouse by train and then we had to change to go to Bath. Then we had to change at Bath to go down to Castle Cary. It took most of the day. But when we got the Morris, even if we only travelled at 40mph, we still did the journey in two hours and in comfort and with all the luggage.'

*Above: The subject of great affection, the car usually became the extra member of the family. This much-loved steed is a 1926 Hudson.*

*Below: Well wrapped-up ladies who lunch take advantage of a folding-down picnic deck.*

*Popular motoring encouraged camping which became quite a fashion before the Second World War. This picture shows nothing less than a rakish SS1 on site. The local four-star hotel must have been full...*

Anthony Wood also clearly recalls how childhood camping trips were made so much easier when they bought their 1925 Rover 10 (for £2.10s) and their Austin 7. 'Having a car gave us a freedom to be able to get away, not only as a family of five, but with our camping gear as well, which you could not have possibly achieved on public transport. There was no public transport leading down to Birling Gap, for example. The nearest you got to there was East Dean, and it would be an awful long way to carry all your bags from there to the campsite.'

Peter Falconer: 'We thoroughly enjoyed camping down by the seaside, especially down at Birling Gap, where you go down on the beach there to the rocks leading round to Beachy Head. Or we'd go down to Goring where there's a long stretch of sand leading out to a shallow sea, so that we could walk out, probably for a quarter of a mile, only up to our knees. And when the tide was out there were many little pools. As kids you always had to rummage around in those for crabs and little fish and so on. It was an awful lot of fun. We started the season each year at Eastertime. We'd pitch a tent at a given site and leave all our gear in it throughout the camping season. Perhaps three of us would be in a tent for ten days or so at a stretch. There was no fear of anyone else coming along and no danger of having your gear interfered with between times.'

### NOT SO HAPPY FOR SOME

Not every child associated motoring with such carefree freedom. Tim Clarke's father was a widowed doctor during the 1920s in Edgehill, and they were living in a 'fairly rural part of Liverpool.' His father's car was one of the first in the area and Tim remembers the back of it like the prison it

was: 'I was about four years old and I recall regularly being scrubbed-up with my sister and being put in the back seat with my three aunts, all spinsters and all dressed in their finery. They'd be taken to various civic functions like the Lord Mayor's Ball, or perhaps to the tennis courts in the Queen's Drive, or the posh shops in Liverpool where we'd sit on little chairs at the side while my aunts tried on innumerable gowns. Then there was coffee in Cardova or the Lyceum Café, with a cream cake which was a treat for being good. My sister and I had to sit there as dolls really – things to be admired; to be seen but not heard.

'I remember the smell of the aunts' perfume very well, a cloying smell that still haunts me. I can vividly remember the little blue bottles with silver lettering on them. 'Evening in Paris' I think it was. I also remember the smell of the leather and wood in our new Vauxhall, and the chauffeur polishing it every day, so you daren't sit in the car with sticky fingers. I recall the sound of the chauffeur cranking the engine to start it, swearing as he couldn't – at least if the aunts weren't around.

'Then there was the sound of the double-declutching and of the horn, sounded as it was on every corner. Using the horn was a status symbol. In fact, our car was a status symbol as far as we were concerned. We'd sit in the back and all the children of the street would come out to have a look. Quite a few of them would throw stones at it or spit at it and things like that...

'Looking back on those days, motoring was a penance for me, not a pleasure or a privilege – my sister and I sitting in the back of the chauffeur-driven car with our dressed-up aunts like mannequins before arriving at some unpleasant destination.'

*Freedom from public transport made camping so much more practical. Journeys that could take a full day might take a fraction the time in the car, and struggling with equipment was a thing of the past.*

## TIM CLARKE REMEMBERS – A MOTORING TRAUMA

*'When I was about eight I experienced the most traumatic experience of my life – a day which is burnt into my memory. I was put into the car, alone with the chauffeur. There was an iron rack on the back of the car and a trunk was strapped onto it along with a wooden box, which I was later to learn was a tuck box. I don't remember anyone waving goodbye to me but we drove off out of Liverpool. I suppose the first few miles were a pleasant experience, being driven alone in the back of a large car. But after a while it began to pall, and after a few hours we stopped at a place which I'd never seen before which was rather like a fort to look at. There the chauffeur unhitched this trunk and the tuck box and put them on the ground. A large lady came out, introduced herself as Matron and told me I was a boarder at the "The Old College, Windermere". The last thing I remember was the chauffeur turning the car round and driving it off onto the gravel. The front of the castle-like building is seared into my memory to this day. I opened the trunk to find it was full of clothes. I often wonder how the governess managed to get them right because I never remember being measured, but there they were, all the right size. And the tears flowed for many days, I can assure you.*

*'I stayed at Windermere for about four years, right through until each summer, because they weren't going to send the chauffeur all that way to fetch us. They used to keep us in school during the shorter holidays – take us up to the Windermere Hotel for our Christmas Party. And come the summer holidays I was put on a train and was met at the Exchange Station in Liverpool by the chauffeur. He would swop my trunk for a case before driving me to Lime Street Station where I was put on to another train to Anglesey where I would stay the whole of my summer holidays with some very nice people. I later came to love them, almost as my grandparents, and I still keep in touch. They're Glenys Kinnock's grandparents, actually.'*

### NOT IN THE WINTER

While Tim Clarke was suffering his aunts' freezing social outings and his father's doctor's rounds, the happy recreational motorist was taking his car off the road for the winter. Tom Swallow recalls: 'Motoring was very much a pleasure activity – most people didn't use the car to go to work. You used the car in the summer for going into the country or the seaside and, as cars were taxed in quarters, it was usual to tax the car only for the two summer quarters. You'd spend the winter fettling the car – doing a decoke, grinding in the valves, doing the kingpins and bushes, that kind of thing – before the next year's 'Glorious 25th' – the 25th of March, which was the first day of the new spring quarter.'

Just starting the car in the winter was a performance, as Rod MacKay recalls: 'Unscrewing the spark plugs, taking them into the house, heating them red-hot over the gas oven, running back to the car, screwing them in, just to get the engine going. There was no such thing as good antifreeze, so having parked the car up on a winter's night, the next thing you had to do was undo the red-hot, muck-covered drain nut under the radiator and let all the water go. Of course the next morning you'd find a miniature skating rink under the car where all the water had settled and frozen. Then you'd put the drain plug in again and run back and forth from the house with kettles of water to fill the radiator up in order to get the car to working temperature.' Thick cold oils also put a heavy strain on self-starters, so it was usually necessary to turn the engine several times with the starting handle before getting into the car, which invariably overheated the driver in his thick coat.

Such a performance, coupled with the many inherent dangers of driving in winter conditions, meant that winter motorists were invariably only those who had to drive as a matter of necessity. Winter motoring was far more hazardous than it is today, with few road markings, no cat's eyes, little grip, poor lights and battery life, and few creature comforts. Tom Swallow recalls taking stacks of hot roast potatoes and a hot water bottle or two with him in the car if he was going on a long trip, just to try to keep warm.

Apart from the cold and slippery conditions, fog was another extremely serious matter. John Marshall writes of a foggy drive he undertook from London to Worthing: 'And though I knew the road far better than any other, I knew it not at all that night, for the most familiar landmarks had vanished or were changed beyond recognition as if by those distorting mirrors at the fair.'

G.R.N. Minchin recalls an astonishing story concerning a young lady, in about 1930, motoring off in the fog after a northern Christmas party in her Austin 7: 'She groped her way along, with visibility nil, when suddenly her car came to a standstill and the front of it went right down. She thought she had run into a ditch, but the front seemed to rise up again and all of a sudden the car shot rapidly backwards. It transpired that she had come upon a travelling circus, the rear of which was brought up by an elephant. She had run into his back legs, causing him to sit down on the car...!'

*How the English middle classes spent their Sundays: Another Standard car attends another picnic which means another photo opportunity. All frightfully jolly.*

## A GREAT CAMARADERIE

For many, motorsport was even more exciting than going to the circus, and so amateur events boomed in Britain during the thirties. Considering how important sports cars became to the British car enthusiast during that period, to say nothing of their importance to the British motor industry, it is remarkable how few provisions existed in this country for motorsport

events. In the thirties only three motor circuits of any note were operating in Britain (excluding the short-lived Isle of Man road course). These were Brooklands, Donington and Crystal Palace.

Furthermore, there was next to no racing car manufacturing. While ERA, MG and Alta made expensive single-seaters in very limited production, the British motorsport movement more commonly relied on special building (using bits from production sports cars) for their single-seater circuit racing, while rich kids tended to buy purpose-built exotics like Maseratis, Bugattis and Alfas from abroad.

Besides, the Brooklands and to a lesser extent the Donington arenas were quite exclusive clubs, while the challenging foreign road races like the Alpine Trial and the Monte Carlo Rally were similarly upper-crust.

For the common man with a sports car to play with, only three practical alternatives existed, trialling, sprinting and hillclimbing, and of those trialling was definitely the favourite. While hillclimbing and sprinting were quite rare events, developed to expensive standards, run on tarmaced surfaces and requiring 'serious' cars, trialling became all the rage in the thirties. In simple terms trialling involved thrashing a perfectly good sports car up a series of hills (the steeper and rougher they were, the better the fun), avoiding rocky outcrops, boulders, ditches, mud pools, trees and anything else that might prove to be an obstacle. Trialling was enjoyable, informal, inexpensive and a great free spectator sport. It was born out of pioneer motoring events (of which the 1000 Mile Trial of 1900 was the first) which were originally designed to test the strength and reliability of production cars. The Motor Cycling Club organised some of the most notorious events, and to this day famous trials such as the Exeter, Land's End, Lakeland and Wessex are run by clubs like the MCC and the Vintage Sports Car Club.

Breakdowns at trials were almost expected, and although the staging of the events caused serious disruptions and traffic jams on the local highways and byways, a great camaraderie was born among the various new motorists.

*Amateur motorsport became enormously popular during the twenties and thirties. Above: A typical twin-cam racing Riley is fettled by two young blades with lighted cigarettes!*

*Below: Rob Walker's Talbot-Lago T150 tackles a hill climb. The Franco-Italian Figoni et Falaschi bodywork was among the most beautiful ever to grace an automobile.*

*Right: a Trojan tackles a popular trial event.*

With so many makes of car on the road, and the cost of motoring very high for the average person, many cars were not in a very good condition. In fact, most of the cars on Britain's roads until the mid-fifties were 'bangers', and before the Second World War the multitude of makes and the various specifications (assuming you hadn't got a newish Austin or a Morris), not to mention the basic nature of the car's mechanisms, meant that a stranded motorist was a by-no-means uncommon

sight. Not everyone was a member of the AA or RAC, and fellow road-users helped each other far more readily than they do today. As Peter Falconer recalls: 'If you stopped on the road you'd be inundated with people offering to help, if the traffic wasn't too heavy. People would always try to please, even tow you to a garage if necessary. It was a very good feeling of having so many friendly people around.'

Brian Asquith from Keighley in West Yorkshire recalls: 'One night in 1935 coming back from Grimsby to Doncaster at about 1am I came across an old Morris 12 on the roadside with its nearside wheel missing. The driver couldn't find the wheel in the dark so I swung my headlights round until we found it – about 100 yards away. Neither the Morris driver nor I had a jack (he hadn't got a spare wheel either) and we couldn't find any of the wheel nuts anywhere. But a lorry came along and, although he didn't have a jack either, he did have a bag of assorted nuts and he was able to find enough of the right size to re-fit the wheel, the three of us lifting up the car between us.'

## TREASURE HUNTS

If trialling was considered all a bit grubby and expensive – if only for the constant car breakages – another new challenge for the sporting motorist was the treasure hunt. These were run by the motoring clubs and charities and involved competitors driving about the countryside in search of clues, a clue found and solved allowing the team to drive on to the next. The first home, having successfully solved all the clues, was declared the winner. Matters were always made more interesting when one car appeared to have solved a clue before another, and so a follow-the-leader scenario might develop, participants hoping to solve the last clue by the time they arrived at the next. That was all well and good, assuming that the pied-piper leader had solved the clue correctly. Far from being pedestrian ambles, treasure hunts became perfect excuses for low-key road-racing, especially if the organisers had been silly enough to provide the clues the night before, thus allowing 'racers' to become familiar with the route in advance. However, the last clue was always retained for the end of the day, so although a mad thrash from the start to the finish was expected, a degree of intellectual challenge was still needed before the competitors settled down in the local public house to recover.

Freddie Passey from Headington in Oxfordshire has memories of good comradeship on the roads during the thirties: 'I was an avid dance-band fan and I was taking my girlfriend and another couple to the Hammersmith Palais in London to see a dance band. About 10 miles into the journey the engine stopped. I lifted the bonnet but didn't have a clue what I was looking for. Then a lorry driver stopped and offered assistance. He fiddled with what I now know to be the distributor and after a few moments gave a triumphant shout, "Ah! It's the make-and-break!"

'A few more moments passed before he asked me to switch on the ignition. Then he gave the starting handle a hefty twirl and presto! the engine fired. I offered him half-a-crown but he refused to accept it.'

*Above: A Riley getting bogged down on a trial event. Horses still had their uses...*
*Below: Traffic jams in and around seaside resorts during the thirties were atrocious as thousands routinely took to the roads at the weekends.*
*Opposite: One of Dunlop's advertisements encompasses all it meant to be a successful sporting motorist.*

### THE ULTIMATE GENTLEMEN

But decency on the roads was a good deal more far-reaching than the kerbside breakdown. Sometime in the late forties Arthur Jeddere-Fisher from Oxford was following a police Wolseley down Park Lane in London when he saw a Bugatti Type 51 (the ultimate Bugatti sports car of its era) in his mirror, trying to pass very fast. Anxious that the police car shouldn't notice it, Arthur zig-zagged across the road in front of the Bugatti. The Bug' slowed and escaped, but Arthur in his Jowett Bradford was consequently pulled over by the police. When the constable accused him of dangerous driving, Arthur, who was destined for an accomplished career in the legal profession, simply reasoned with him that he was trying to prevent a fellow motorist from committing a crime. He was let off accordingly!

In his fun-filled book of motoring memories, *Recreation Motoring*, John Marshall recalls another Park Lane incident: 'Just as I was accelerating for the desperate dash down the boiling centre current, a person so foolhardy that he surely could not have survived for long, attempted to ford the main stream. I jammed on the brakes and there was a nasty jolt at my rear as the

Above: An idyllic
early-thirties suburban
scene is the backdrop
for the elegant lady
Morris driver.

Right: The 1954 Austin
A30, Britain's best-loved
small car before the
coming of the Mini, and
the spiritual successor of
the original Austin 7.

maniac vanished... Within seconds the constable had materialised, as they so miraculously do. This officer said to me: "I saw it all, sir. It was not your fault and if any insurance is involved there will be a report to that effect." At the same time the driver of the car which had run into my stern apologised and I could do no less than assure him that he could not help it either.

'"Should we exchange cards?"

'"But certainly."

'Should I subsequently discover any damage would I please send the bill to him? But yes, he insisted.

'Three months later when I had completely forgotten the incident there was a phone call to my office from this motorist who had inadvertently collided with me. But really, he had become worried. There had been no bill from me for the damage. He thought perhaps that I had lost his card.'

Perhaps John Marshall's delightful story of that motorist's integrity sums up the changing face of motoring and the freedom of the road during the fifties: a time when chivalry among the knights of the road was dwindling, the selfish motorist was gaining prominence, and traffic was becoming a 'terrifying swirl' of being 'hooted, hounded, harried and hustled'.

*The Morris Minor in desirable 'tourer' form. Seen for the first time at the 1948 Motor Show, the Minor was, like the Mini, Alec Issigonis's creation. It was designed to be Britain's 'people's car' and, thanks to its near cult following, it was to remain in production until the early seventies.*

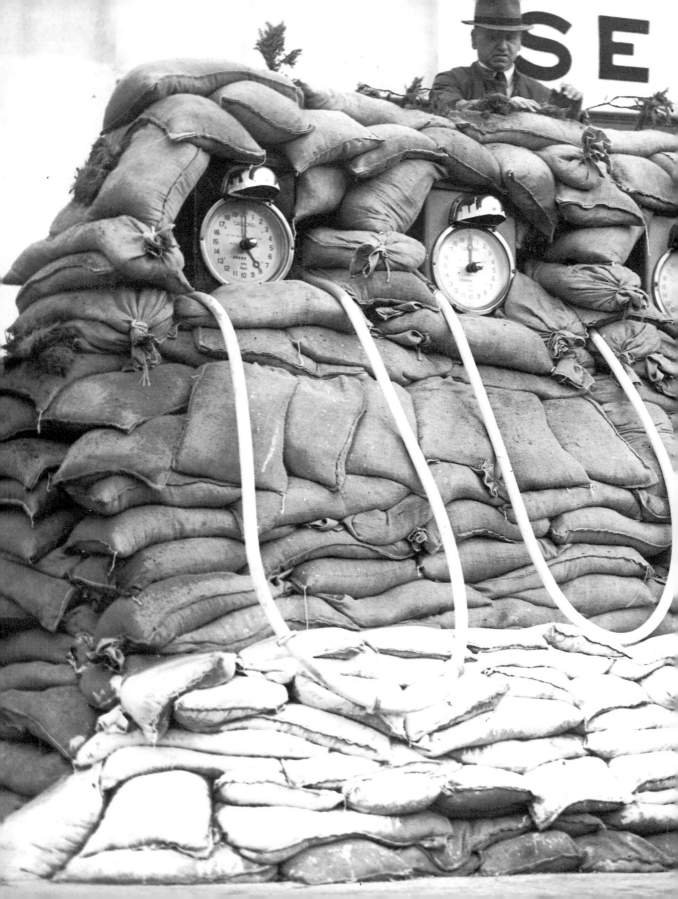

Chapter 4

# THE AUSTERITY YEARS

W hile Britain had experienced austerity motoring during the First World War, the trebling of car taxes, doubling of petrol tax and, later, rationing of fuel barely affected the general population. Not only were there far fewer motor cars on the roads in those days, but the restrictions on motoring enforced by the government were only instituted in 1916 and were repealed as soon as the war was over two years later. However, the austerity years brought about by the Second World War lasted for over a decade and affected much of the population: both those who personally motored and those who relied on motors to support their businesses or services.

By the late 1930s the motor car had become a symbol of freedom for Britain's middle classes, and as Andrew Lane reminds us in his book *Austerity Motoring*: 'There was something special about August Bank Holiday 1939. It seemed that all the cars in Britain, two million of them, were on the roads. The car trippers that weekend feared that this could be their last chance of pleasure motoring before the inevitable war began.' War was declared on 3rd September 1939, and petrol rationing was instigated a few days later. Austerity motoring had begun.

### THE PETROL RATION

Initially, private motoring was not banned, and a basic petrol ration was available, allowing around 200 miles of motoring per motorist per month. This aim was roughly achieved by allowing motorcycles a ration of 2 gallons a month, then 4 gallons for cars of up to 7hp, 5 gallons for 8 and 9hp cars, the ration rising progressively from there and peaking at 10 gallons for cars of 20hp or more. Rations were controlled through the issue of coupons.

At the same time that petrol rationing was instigated, the government decreed that all brands of petrol should be pooled and that only one basic petrol should be available. 'Pool' was 'always appalling' in the words of Peter Falconer, but it came in two principal types: the clear variety, which the private motorist was allowed to use, and another version dyed pink, which was made exclusively available (and in much more generous quantities) to the military and drivers of commercial vehicles. However, a pink surplus was never particularly hard to find and so a black market readily developed for it. 'Pool' wasn't expensive petrol at 1s 6d a gallon, but the price of it did fluctuate a certain amount, rising to as high as 2s 1/2d in 1942. Black market petrol was usually three times the price.

*Pages 110-111: Petrol pumps during the black-out are heavily protected by sand bags.*

*Below: A 1909/10 Riley 10hp being used on military manoeuvres during the First World War. Mechanised transport was all but non-existent in the army when the war began.*

The basic petrol ration allowance could be supplemented by any number of special allowances. These ranged from those applicable to motorists working in the 'essential' services, to allowances such as those made to motorists who might volunteer the use of their car for the transport of servicemen home or to take others to their workplaces. While crucial professionals such as doctors, farmers and those in the haulage trades received among the most generous fuel allowances, many other special cases existed, all of which were subject to individual application and assessment. Architects and chaplains, the Home Guard and prisoners of war returning to Britain, mothers taking

*Above: The first day of 'Pool' spirit distribution. The price is 1s 6d a gallon and the day is 5th September 1939.*

*Left: Zenith carburettors find good cause to advertise now that the car has become an essential wartime tool.*

their children to school, those who offered to take evacuees to their new homes, or relatives to meet their injured sons in hospital – all could have secured additional petrol allowances. How austere your motoring was therefore depended both on what you did and whom you knew – at least until July 1942. From then on, the basic ration was abolished altogether and it wasn't reinstated until after the war. In the meantime, stricter allowance schemes and black market purchases were likely to be the only means by which to obtain petrol.

'There were usually ways by which you could drive or ride in the war,' explains Peter Falconer. 'If you were in the construction industry, as I was, you drove cars right through the war on special allowances. Construction workers built airfields, factories... I was involved with converting factories in Gloucester and Cheltenham for the production of war hardware. Furthermore, driving conditions during the daytime were excellent. There was no traffic to speak of, at least until the Americans arrived, and there were no speed limits whatsoever, so you could do some remarkable runs. I remember going from Cheltenham to Marble Arch in 92 minutes... and it wasn't illegal!'

*An Austin falls victim to an air raid in London's Leicester Square.*

Others obtained extra fuel more by luck than design. Ralph Lee remembers: 'A British fighter came down near where we were living in a caravan. It was having engine trouble so had to make an emergency landing. Having gone to meet the pilot we thought we'd borrow his petrol. It was green, so you didn't want to be caught with it, but we got rid of it quick enough.'

James Lazenby was rather more enterprising: 'There were all sorts of things you could swop for fuel. For example, a local farmer might have killed a sheep and you might take it to the local aerodrome's mess and trade it for some fuel. There was a black market in most things, except the things you just never saw, bananas, sweets, things like that. Farmers had very large petrol allocations, especially during harvest time to fuel the combine harvesters that the Americans had introduced. If the farmers didn't use up their quota by the end of the 3-month period then there were plenty of coupons available to trade. You could always buy them at the pub, albeit at a price.' James and his father ran taxis during the war which were soon deemed essential, not only by local people

*Above: Many women learnt to drive during the Second World War, which did an enormous amount to quash prejudice against them. These are WATS troops on convoy duty.*

*Left: It was incredible, and it would be as popular after the war as it was during it. The ubiquitous Jeep shows its paces.*

who laid their cars up after the loss of the basic petrol ration, but also by the newly arrived Americans who were otherwise stranded at nearby RAF Riddington. 'I was 17 when the Americans arrived, 6000 of them at the local base, and it wasn't unusual to see a rather large petrol tanker backing into my father's yard, sent down by the local GIs to keep the taxis running. Up at the aerodrome on the flat ground the last 50 or so gallons wouldn't come out, but on the yard's slope it would alright!'

### ALTERNATIVE MEANS

With such drastic petrol restrictions, alternative fuels, particularly producer gas, played a much more important, although still restricted, role in Britain's motoring. Gas had already proved viable as a fuel during the First World War, especially in cities where the mileages motorists needed to cover tended to be smaller and gas supplies were more readily available. During the Second World War the advantage of gas was less marked. Cars were generally a good deal faster by the 1940s than they had been in

*Right: Fuel rationing meant being resourceful. This handsome 1942 1hp équipe looks particularly well presented.*

*Opposite, top: If there's no petrol for the car, simply put the chauffeur on tandem duty.*

Edwardian times, and the statutory 50 per cent performance reduction when running on gas was far more noticeable on a modern car at that time.

For those who did opt for a gas conversion, two fuel supply options existed: either the gas could be collected from the local gas suppliers, where it would be piped into a large storage bag mounted precariously on the roof of the car, or it could be produced by a gas plant actually fitted to the car in question. The latter was a bulky affair, either strapped onto the back of the car or carried behind on a trailer, and required fuelling with coal, wood, chicken droppings or whatever it was designed to process. Either bag or manufacturing plant

solutions were incongruous, precarious and highly inefficient. Although the bagging method was cheaper, a bag's contents would only last 20–30 miles, which didn't give such a vehicle a very useful range. The on-car plant method was a whole lot more expensive, even if the fuel range was four or five times as great. Those who invested in gas conversions were frequently disenchanted. Red Daniells remembers: 'I had two friends who converted their cars to gas power, carrying a huge dirigible full of gas on the tops of their cars. They were convinced that it was going to be the answer to the petrol shortage, but neither were very enthusiastic after they'd tried it.'

A much more common solution to extending one's motoring range was the illegal practice of mixing paraffin in with 'Pool' petrol. 'There was no tax on paraffin,' remembers Tom Swallow, 'so you could be pinched for avoiding fuel tax.' It was also near-impossible to start most cars with paraffin, so a somewhat complicated procedure was required. Peter Falconer recalls: 'You had to start the car on

## AN AUSTIN FOR £1.10S

In 1939 G.L. Barron (then of east London) received his call-up papers. Being a qualified engineer he was offered a post in Eastleigh, working on radar-protection technology. Newly married, and with a new commute, Mr Barron needed a car. 'Looking around local scrap yards I found an old Austin 7 which had clocked up over 100,000... It ran well, even if it was a bit noisy and after a lot of bargaining I paid £1.10s for it. Almost every fortnight my wife and I drove the Austin to east London to visit parents and relatives, and the car endured many air-raids. To supplement the fuel I added paraffin and other solvents, so it often used to stop at roundabouts because it had overheated, but over the next four years the Austin never let me down. Eventually I managed to sell it for £6.'

pure petrol but could then switch to the paraffin mixture once the engine was running hot. The car would then run quite satisfactorily, but if you had to re-start the engine the pure petrol supply had to be reattached.' James Lazenby remembers: 'It was pretty common practice to see just how much paraffin you could add to a gallon of petrol for the vehicle still to start.'

Using paraffin was a risky business, though, because the exhaust of a paraffin-fuelled vehicle was very distinctive. Lazenby: 'Paraffin created an awful exhaust smoke and stink. Everyone could see who was running a half paraffin mixture for the clouds of smoke. Tractor Vapourising Oil, which was a type of paraffin, was also mixed in illegally and even aircraft fuel was employed. With some paraffin added into that, the octane levels would be brought down. Running neat aircraft fuel was a bad idea as it would burn your engine valves out absolutely within a few miles.'

Less risky than running fuel mixtures was to obtain 'pink' petrol on the black market and remove the dye. Red Daniells was a non-commissioned officer during the war and his driver told him how it was done: 'Add two aspirins per gallon, leave it to precipitate, the dye all falls to the bottom and you can then pour most of the clear petrol off.' The other alternative, explains Daniells, 'was to pour the dyed petrol through a carbon-granule

*The gaseous options: as stored in a large roof-mounted bag (opposite) or as produced on-site (below), in this case piped from a trailer to a Ford V8. Neither arrangement proved very successful.*

gas mask, which was also available on the black market. It required patience but you'd end up with a palish-looking fuel. I presume if you did the aspirin trick as well you'll have ended up with the really pure stuff.'

### THE SPARES CRISIS

Fuel rationing was only part of the war-time motorist's problems. Spare parts and, most significantly, consumables, were rarely obtainable, and legislation ensured that black markets in such items were kept to a minimum. Tyres became almost unobtainable after Malaya, the rubber-supplying nation, was lost to the Japanese in 1942, and one could not sell secondhand tyres, for example, unless they came on the car to which they were fitted. To obtain a new tyre or bearings required a special application to the government. Those not motoring for the most essential services need not bother to apply.

*WAAFs fuelling the staff car. Women drivers were so rare before the Second World War that ladies driving at night were assumed to be 'on the game'.*

Peter Falconer was a member of the Home Guard during the War and remembers: 'If you were in the Home Guard then motoring was a lot easier. If you were short of anything for your car you could often find someone in the Home Guard who would make it for you, or who could get it. This was largely because the factories would sometimes suffer slack periods while they waited for raw materials. During these periods workers would produce all manner of things. You could go to a Home Guard meeting one evening, place your order for, say, a piston, and take delivery of a first-class item perhaps the next day, and made out of the highest quality materials. They seemed to be able to achieve anything in the Home Guard and, of course, the camaraderie went on long after the War. The Home Guard Motor Cycle Club, for example, survived well into the fifties, perhaps even the sixties.'

*Sensational evidence from 1939 of a 4.5-litre Bentley which has been converted into a fire tender for the Chichester Fire Brigade. The driver doesn't look smug for nothing.*

James Lazenby was in no better position as a garage owner to acquire spares than most other motorists. 'One chap in our village stuffed the tyres of his Austin 7 with hay in order to squeeze more life out of them. Another way to keep your tyres useable was to get an old worn-out tyre the next size up from yours and put it on the outside of your tyre. So if you had a 17-inch wheel you put an 18-inch tyre on the outside of your 17-inch tyre. It flapped away but you still got along with it. Of course, this was a long time before the MoT!'

### ALL BLACKED-OUT

While keeping the car on the road was challenge enough, driving was more hazardous than it had ever been. Road accident figures peaked during the Second World War, achieving levels never again witnessed, irrespective of the density of cars on Britain's roads. The reason was the 'black-out'.

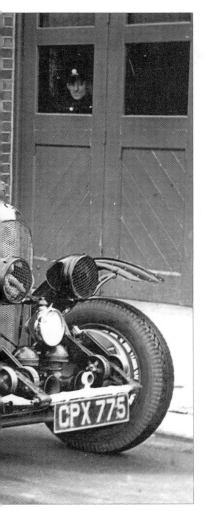

The 'black-out' was the term given to the legal requirement to extinguish lights after dark to prevent enemy aircraft from identifying built-up areas. A practice 'black-out' was run in central, southern and eastern England over 9th–10th August 1939. In the words of Andrew Lane: 'In preparation for this, everything solid bordering a roadway was painted either completely white or with white stripes. Trees, lamp posts, kerbs, traffic lights, bollards and Belisha beacons all received the white-wash treatment.'

Such preparations gave the motorist a sporting chance of not hitting anything in the absence of street lighting. This became especially important after headlight masks were introduced soon after war was declared. These had to be fitted over one of the car's headlights, while the other (on two-headlight vehicles) had its bulb removed. All light reflectors had to be blackened or removed. Rear lights were painted over or had a piece of newspaper fitted behind their lenses to restrict the light emitted. At the same time that masking was instigated, another ruling meant that all running-board edges and bumpers had to be painted white.

*Below: Headlight masks were required to cover one headlight on all vehicles during the black-out. In addition, the bulb had to be removed from the second headlight and reflectors removed from both.*

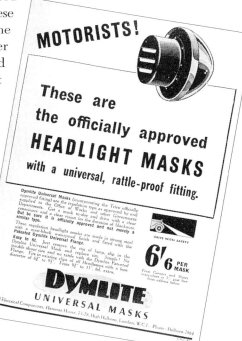

Peter Falconer remembers: 'Right from the start you had to fit a mask over one headlight which was faced with louvres which were cut downwards at about 45 degrees. The light that penetrated was minimal and you could never see a vehicle coming towards you. I used to pray for moonlight otherwise driving was lethal – like motoring in a constant thick fog. Halfway through the war they altered the mask design so that a flap could be pulled up to sit at 90 degrees to the upright part of the mask. This revised design did let some light onto the road and you might see for about 30 feet in front of you, but it was still very dangerous. Several people were killed in the Home Guard alone from running into obstructions.'

Tom Swallow was lucky to survive a motorcycle accident during the black-out after he and a friend on a side-car combination hit a kerb and were hurled over the handlebars: 'It was a very dangerous thing, driving in the black-out. You certainly didn't go out unless you had to. There were a lot of accidents, particularly with motorcycles hitting the kerbs and the riders being thrown from their machines. There was no such thing as reflective paint in those days, and cat's eyes came about later on.'

Just how dangerous black-out driving was can be gauged by the accident figures of the time which rose by 20 per cent in 1939 to a total of 8272, despite less than half the year being affected by the black-out regulations. The following year the accident rate soared again, even though a 20mph speed limit had been introduced, and peaked in 1941 at 9169 road deaths, including 4781 pedestrians. That figure was 38 per cent higher than the immediate pre-war figure, despite there being well under half the cars on the roads.

The road-death toll was just one of the many reasons that the policy of advancing the clocks by one hour was introduced. British Summertime began in February 1940 (Double British Summertime was instigated during the course of 1941), which goes some way to helping us understand why this misnomer remains with us. Advancing the clock by one hour effectively kept roads light for an hour longer during the working day: there was one hour less in the day during which motorists and pedestrians were at risk.

The summer of 1940 also witnessed the taking down of road signs as the threat of an enemy invasion became more real. Some beaches were closed to the public; check-points were set up at which motorists were forced to stop; and cars had to be immobilised when they were left. Immobilising usually

## TIM CLARKE REMEMBERS – DRIVING AN AMBULANCE IN THE BLACK-OUT

*'Driving an ambulance was a very unnerving experience. Everything was blacked-out, of course, and your covered headlights only provided a narrow slit of light which didn't really illuminate anything. There were no street lights to show you where to go, so you couldn't drive very fast. When approaching a bombed area there were all kinds of casualties around, from people coming out of buildings badly dazed to bricks and rubble all over the ground. Sometimes it felt more like driving a tank than an ordinary road vehicle. Of course, having arrived at the scene, you then had to get out of there again to go to the hospital, which may then be full so sometimes you had to drive on to another. The sky was often illuminated by the fires and incendiary bombs: you could be driving along one minute in pitch darkness and the next the scene could be lit up by a beautiful incendiary. Then there were the flashes of anti-aircraft guns, but they didn't provide much useful illumination to the driver. There was a big anti-aircraft battery in Botanic Park where we lived, and when those guns were all firing and the searchlights were blazing there would be a lot of light, but not the kind you can drive by. One flash of such light and your eyes are blinded and you can't see where you're going for the next minute. So driving was very hazardous. You had to wear your tin hat, not least because of all the shrapnel flying around, and you had to keep your gas mask at the ready and be prepared to jump out at any moment when a warden shouted to you that there was a bomb.'*

*Left: A stretcher party and their mount. Note that the edges of the wings are painted white. This was black-out regulation decor.*

*Below: The royal Daimler sports full black-out regalia, although privilege clearly allows two headlight masks instead of one.*

Men who design finer and faster machines choose this car for their own use

BY APPOINTMENT

Daimler

involved the removal of the distributor's rotor arm ('The fact that enemy paratroopers dropping in might also have had Lucas rotor arms didn't seem to matter,' remembers Red Daniells) or, less commonly, chaining the car's wheels through their spokes. The winter of 1940 was particularly hard, and most motorists laid up their cars for the war's duration, defeated by a combination of the black-out, lack of fuel and spares, and the weather.

## MANUFACTURING FOR THE WAR

As early as 1936 the government had assessed the design and manufacturing capabilities of the motor industry and had implemented factory construction programmes to facilitate mass aircraft and munitions manufacture. As Andrew Lane reminds us in his book *Austerity Motoring*: 'In early 1940 there were still on average 3500 new registrations a month and there were still 130 models available. The car manufacturers were instructed by the government to continue production for the export market. So from October 1939 to May 1940 an average of 5000 cars a month was exported. Ford even announced a new model, the Anglia, but production was short-lived.'

Although England's major motor manufacturers continued making cars until about the middle of 1941, purchasing one was not easy and became all but impossible for a year after July 1940 when the government took control over new car stocks. For 12 months no private motorist was able to buy a car, before the government revised its rules to allow private individuals involved in essential business – doctors, for example – to buy new cars from July 1941, albeit subject to the new purchase tax which

*Left: To emphasise the respectability of their product, Daimler ran a series of advertisements during the War years showing senior military figures using their wares.*

*Above: Vauxhall Motors designed and built the Churchill tank in one year.*

### LOSING HIS CAR IN THE WAR

For those who motored before the war, the inflated prices of post-war cars seemed particularly unreasonable. William Roe from Chiswick recalls: 'I purchased my 1936 Morris 8 saloon early in 1942, but it wasn't long before petrol rationing ended and no petrol was made available to private motorists at all. So my father jacked up the Morris 8 on blocks in the garage-workshop at the bottom of his garden, where it perished following the dropping of incendiary bombs. When I returned to civilian life in the summer of 1946, I had no car and only £25 from the War Damage Commission as compensation for the loss of my Morris 8. I had to find ten times that amount to acquire a second-hand 1932 Austin 7, a result of there being no new cars available to civilians other than those in "reserved occupations". They were able to sell their cars at a figure which was well in excess of the sum they had paid for the car when new.'

was levied at 33.3 per cent for cars up to £1000 in price and at a massive 66.6 per cent for new cars sold for more. For this reason the big manufacturers kept up a trickle production of low horse-power, low-cost models, but volume car production was to cease until the war was over.

## No early reprieve

In many respects, the hardships of the post-war motorist were worse than they had been in wartime. When the war was finally won Britain was virtually bankrupt, and the Labour Government chose to continue the years of austerity in a vigorous attempt to minimise inflation, and to pour all the nation's limited resources into goods produced for export. Foremost among the exporting industries was the motor industry, and so troops returning home to their war-weary families had many of their dreams of peacetime freedom dashed: rationing would continue, and would do so for many years.

Tom Swallow was a prisoner of war, returning home in June 1945. 'We had hoped, of course, that we were coming back to a free world of motoring but that was a forlorn hope – everything was rationed. Food rationing was worse after the war than it was during it in many respects. I was fortunate because, being a prisoner of war I was given a fuel allowance when I returned home – so that I could visit my family and old friends – to give me a little bit of freedom. I had the use of the family car, a little Wolseley Hornet, and so one day six of us crowded into it with two or three tents, cooking equipment and food. We set off from Birmingham to Brixham and got just beyond Weston-super-Mare when we got a puncture. Not having a spare, we got in touch with my mother who contacted the Ministry of Transport to obtain a permit for a new tyre which we eventually collected from the station and fitted to the car. We camped for three days in a farmer's field while we waited! But I was much more fortunate than most. I decided to start a taxi business using the Wolseley with my brother-in-law. I applied for a petrol ration, quoting my prisoner-of-war service and, luckily, was given enough to start the business. I recollect one trip I did from just outside Dudley Castle. Charging half-a-crown apiece, I got home and found I had 12 pieces, which meant I must have had 12 passengers in, or on, the little four-seater. But there was no option. There was no other transport. It was either me or they'd have to walk miles and miles.'

Now the war was over, getting around petrol rationing was considered fair game. The paraffin and TVO mixtures remained, while those running higher compression engines experimented with methanol mixtures. Tom Swallow, anxious to gain an anti-knock fuel for

*A suitably chirpy Group Captain Scroggs with his 1927 Trojan at the first post-war British motoring event, at Wrotham Park, June 1945.*

his competition motorcycle, even persuaded a chemist at the local National Tar Distillery (which produced the National Benzole Petrol) to supply him with a special 'recipe'. 'The basis of it was wood naphtha which they produced in large quantities at the distillery and there were a few other ingredients, the main being methylated spirits and mothballs! It worked, but it was very, very hot and burnt the engine valves very quickly...'

Ralph Lee, a Londoner at the time recalls: 'I used to go for my lunch to a pub in Chelsea every day where there were a crowd of people who all had their fingers in something. The greengrocer, for example, would ask how I was off for coal, and if I said I was a bit short then he'd pop round and shoot some through my hatch in the pavement outside the house. And the landlord might come up to me and whisper, "I've just put a couple of gallons in your tank." I don't know where he got it from.'

Red Daniells recalled: 'I came home after the war and found that not only was a car valuable but that its petrol was even more so. I have clear memories of people scurrying around with 4½ gallons of petrol in jerry cans. You went down to Victoria at dusk and the lorry drivers who still had lorries that ran on petrol (rather than diesel) were happy to cream off some of the fuel, which they then sold at enormous prices, like 3s 6d a gallon.'

*It's 1944 and road signs are being re-erected. They had been removed during the early days of the war as a precaution in case of invasion.*

## EXPORT OR DIE

Needless to say, post-war car production resumed as soon as raw material supplies allowed, but still using the tooling that was available before war broke out.

The new designs that had been worked on during the war were not yet ready for production and so the immediate post-war car looked identical to the pre-war variety. Austin, Ford, Morris, Vauxhall, MG and the like immediately commenced manufacture of their pre-war models, although the Ford Anglia seemed the freshest of the set and the cheapest too, at £293 plus £64 new purchase tax. Humber cheekily launched the new Hawk in 1945, which was actually a pre-war Hillman 14 with hydraulic brakes and various extra trimmings. The new Snipe and Super Snipe were six-cylinder versions of the same car, but Humber staff cars had built up a true-Brit wartime reputation and Humber badges had a certain status. The 'proper' Humber staff car was also available, but called a Pullman, and with a body

*Export or die. Morrises are prepared for export to Hindustan. Fifty per cent of all cars produced had to be sold abroad.*

coach-built by firms like Thrupp and Maberly (who bodied a lot of military cars during the war) or H.J. Mulliner.

Armstrong-Siddeley were in the extremely fortunate position of having cars ready for production because they had originally been envisaged for a 1940–41 launch. They therefore introduced all-new cars the moment that VE-Day was announced. The Lancaster saloon, the Hurricane cabriolet and the Typhoon coupé all patriotically borrowed the names of British military aircraft built partly by Armstrong-Siddeley during the war. Armstrong-Siddeley's technical rival, SS Cars, very sensibly renamed its cars Jaguars, after their successful pre-War sporting models.

Most other luxury car manufacturers in Britain had little hope of selling their new wares until the vicious 66.6 per cent purchase tax applicable to cars selling for over £1000 was abolished. Jensen could produce just 15 examples of their new PW between 1946 and 1951, and the splendid Invicta Black Prince brought the famous company to its knees after only 25 examples were built between 1946 and 1950 for the same reason. Rolls-Royce and Bentley were in a stronger financial position than most, following their successful war contracts designing and building military engines. The new Bentley Mk VI, although launched in 1946, went on to sell over 5000 examples until its demise in 1952. But such luxury car success stories were few.

Other manufacturers that survived the period did so either through exceptional technical merit (as was the case with the sensational Bristol 400 of 1947 and the intelligent Gerald Palmer-designed Jowett Javelin), or through clever styling for the export market (as with the Austin Atlantic), or by partial redesign using old model parts (as was the case with the capable Ford V8 Pilot of 1947 and the handsome Palmer-designed Riley RM series cars from 1946).

Gerald Palmer was arguably the greatest of Britain's production car designers of the era. Having gone to Jowett during the War to tell them what he thought the ideal post-War car should be, he was given the contract to design it single-handedly. It was a revolutionary car in its day. Palmer told me: 'There were certain design priorities, namely a rugged but lightweight build, a high ground clearance, compactness throughout, the ability to access the car from either side, which meant dispensing with the common transmission tunnel, and I felt that a heater and radio should be standard equipment.' But great as the Javelin was, Jowett had difficulty making enough cars. Palmer remembers: 'One of the biggest problems we had in those days was getting hold of the raw materials. The government would only allocate materials depending on how many cars their assessors felt would be exported. Unfortunately, Jowett did not have much of an export market before the war so the company didn't have the credibility to gain a large enough raw material quota after it. We even looked at making the Javelin out of plastic at one time to get round the problem.'

Having spent much of his life in South Africa, Palmer knew how rugged and reliable a car would have to be to survive the export market. 'A lot of the early post-war cars were not designed, tested or developed as they should have been,' he explains, 'and the result of that was that many British cars gained a poor reliability reputation abroad. They simply were not up to the task.' It was a fact that few other manufacturers appreciated and which was to cost the industry dearly by the 1950s.

Straight after the war the government told car manufacturers that 50 per cent of their output had to be exported, and by 1947, with Britain's economic situation worsening, the export quota was raised to a crippling 75 per cent of production. To make matters worse, early 1947 witnessed the harshest winter ever recorded in Britain, so compounding the misery brought about by continued rationing of food, clothing, soap, fuels and other essentials. There was deep dissatisfaction throughout the country, as

*The American influence on styling is clear in this Austin A90 Atlantic, produced specifically with high Stateside sales in mind.*

there seemed little reason for continuing such extreme austerity: it was as if the Labour Government was determined that the British people should pay for the war through an almost puritanical suffering, denying themselves any luxuries for the sake of the national good. The government argued that petrol was bought in US dollars, and dollars had to be conserved, but, as the author Andrew Lane points out: 'Motorists asked why, if dollars were in short supply, was there no restriction on the £30 million spent on tobacco imports and the £19 million spent on American films?'

Crippled under the ever-more demanding export drive, the British despaired in August 1947 when even the basic fuel ration was abolished and petrol allocations were restored to almost the worst levels of the war. Despite John Cobb breaking the land-speed record in his Napier-Railton at 394mph and the announcement of the sensational BRM V16 as Britain's new Grand Prix racing car, motoring in Britain had never seemed more bleak.

After vigorous campaigning by the press and motoring organisations, the basic petrol ration was reintroduced almost a year later, and at a substantially lower level than before, allowing under 100 miles a month of motoring in an economical car. And all this only months before the 1948 Motor Show, which was to display the finest selection of all-new British cars ever seen.

*Gerald Palmer's outstanding Jowett Javelin. Despite its many abilities, shortages in raw materials and a weak overseas sales network eventually forced the company out of business in 1954.*

## A GREATER DEMAND

Despite fluctuating petrol rationing regulations, the car was the ultimate symbol of freedom to the common man after the war, and demand for cars far outstripped supply. Unlike the First World War, the second one had been heavily mechanised, and many a soldier had discovered the thrill of driving at least a motorcycle, if not jeeps, trucks and staff cars, during his or her military service.

With people having a little money to spend and a renewed zest for life, to say nothing of the possible need to commute from the newly developing suburbs, cars were desperately desired. It was inevitable that secondhand cars could frequently be sold for much higher prices than their unavailable new equivalents. 'You couldn't get new cars for love nor money,' recalls Peter Falconer, 'although you could if you were a doctor. In fact, doctors would become motor traders, because that's how they could make money.' New cars could immediately be re-sold for prices much higher than those for which they had been purchased. In July 1946 the government introduced legislation which forced the rare eligible purchaser of a new car to keep it for at least a six-month period. The following year this period became extended to a year, and in 1950 a two-year 'no sell' rule was implemented. This initiative did much to curb profiteering by those in the privileged position of being qualified to buy new cars, but did nevertheless mean that those who secured new cars could still profit handsomely from selling them after they had owned them for the necessary length of time. 'Several relations of mine were doctors,' Peter Falconer continued, 'and they thought it was a wonderful arrangement.'

Anthony Wood remembers: 'My in-laws paid about £300 for a 1937 Morris 8 soon after the end of the War, yet by that time it was nearly ten years old.' The list price for a new Morris 8 in 1946 was little more than £300, and a nearly-new model might sell for 50–80 per cent more. Many three-year-old cars in 1949 were still selling for their 1946 list prices.

For most, however, a new car was available only if you had the patience. James Lazenby: 'It was a matter of putting your name down on a waiting list and then probably having to wait three or four years. There was a lot of jealousy because of that, especially if you were a garage proprietor, as I was. There were some clients who couldn't see why I should have a car when they hadn't got one.' Ralph Lee had always bought his Standard cars direct from the Standard factory before the War and so had his name on the

*Jaguar cars sold particularly well abroad. Here the new post-war Mk V saloons prepare to hit the road in 1949.*

## RED DANIELLS REMEMBERS – THE MOTOR TRADE SPIV

'The spiv – the shark performer of the motor trade – was a thoroughly reprehensible individual during the last years of the War. He wasn't regarded as funny, because he was perceived to be unpatriotic. But in the later Forties and early Fifties the spiv with his small moustache, side-boards, coat with the collar turned up, always looking about, was much more amusing. He could be selling fruit in the West End from a barrow or dodgy motors at night under a street lamp in the rain (that's when the secondhand motor car looks its best). The image did change because spivs found that their attire led to a sort of unrest among the people with whom they were dealing. They eventually found it better if they could manage to look like, say, an off-duty bishop. This resulted in the unctuous and portly spivs of Fitzroy Square appearing almost benevolent – everyone was to prefer being swindled by people like that. You could identify the early spiv from his black full-length coat, usually sitting just three inches from the ground. The late comedian Sid Field used to do a spiv character called Slasher Green who was dressed just like that and Slasher used to make the Prince of Wales theatre roar with laughter, because outside there were identical people selling fruit 'n' veg, all dressed in those long black coats. So the coat got a bad reputation and was dressed up with camel hair around the shoulders, with a paisley scarf, sometimes even a Homburg. But the spiv could seldom manage the facial rectitude that goes with the Homburg, so they always looked like a fairly shifty bunch of bank under-managers. The wider trouser bottom on suits was significant because rationing dictated that only 17 inches was possible in the cloth, so the 22-inch trouser bottom showed you'd got contacts and coupons galore. Spivs like these circulated in the area of Warren Street and Fitzroy Square where there were more smartly dishonest people to the square foot than I think I've ever seen anywhere else, except possibly in Berlin.'

waiting list for a new model when War broke out. 'They rang me up soon after the War and asked me if I still wanted a new car. I mean, new cars were like gold dust! They said they had two for sale, one with a heater and one with a radio, both new ideas at the time. I reasoned that I could build myself a radio in due time, but I couldn't make myself a heater, so I opted for the heated car... We'd go shopping in this new car – a Vanguard – and when we came back with our packages we couldn't get into the car for people surrounding it, mostly men, all having a good look.'

Without new cars to buy, the motorist had to look either to the various auctions of used military vehicles to find transport, or to the secondhand car market. Skulduggery was rife in both arenas, but particularly in less intimate city communities where motor trade spivs gained a fearsome reputation for selling dreadful cars for greatly inflated prices. Much of this dishonesty was born out of the fact that spare parts were so hard to find that purchasers expected to buy a car with some faults. Radiators filled with porridge or raw eggs to stop them leaking (Red Daniells remembers one or two he found filled with concrete!), and sawdust or diced corks put in gearboxes to stop them whining, were recognised 'bodges'.

Garage owner Arthur Walker has memories of one car he repaired with its floor made out of biscuit tins and of another which he found using curdled cow's milk as brake fluid. However, as Red Daniells explains: 'There weren't so many crooked deals to make a car run because if you could make it go for 50 yards then it would probably run for 5 miles which had to be inside the terms of the deal. Of course, if you wanted to be more sure of what you bought you had to have the money and then you could go to the top end of the motor trade hierarchy: to the chinless idiots operating in Regent Street and Bond Street, people with public-school educations and voices to match who sold motor cars to their peers. It was enormous fun listening to these people because they knew little about cars – very much a case of the blind leading the blind. But these people wore blazers and allowed the customer a trial run, which at least meant that the motor offered was actually motorable.'

At the bottom end of the trade hierarchy was the motor auction. Peter Falconer remembers: 'There were a lot of auctions immediately after the war so that the Ministry of Defence could get rid of those vehicles which they had requisitioned at the beginning of the war. The black marketeers, who had made cash during the war, went to town at these sales, buying huge quantities of vehicles. But if you bought a car at auction the chance of getting it home under its own power was very remote.' Auctions were also used to acquire valuable spare parts, but these were often sold in batches in such a way as to force the purchaser to buy a lot of other things he didn't want as part of the job lot. Red Daniells: 'I remember a motor trader here in South London who had to buy the gun turret blister off a Hampton bomber and some retractable landing gear just to get a box of clutch plates. The shortage of spares led to a whole new culture of traders who would supply spares which either weren't needed for the customer's car in the first place or which didn't fit.'

## MOTOR SHOW!

In the midst of the strictest rationing regulations and highly restricted domestic new car sales came the 1948 Motor Show. The show attracted record crowds of more than 560,000 people to view more than 20 new models exhibited. The stars of the show were undoubtedly the innovative new 'car for the people', Alec Issigonis's Morris Minor, and the sensational new Jaguar XK120 sports car.

*You could look but you couldn't buy. Even if these sensational Daimlers were not destined for export, a 66.6 per cent purchase tax on cars priced at more than £1000 ensured that British domestic luxury car sales were minimal.*

## DISMISSING THE BEETLE

The British missed an opportunity to make dramatic progress in motor manufacturing after the Second World War when allied motor-industry assessors, Henry Ford II among them, dismissed the Volkswagen Beetle as a car with no future. The British statement regarding the Beetle, which was in production by 1945, stated: 'This car does not fulfil the technical requirements which must be expected from a motor car. Its performance and qualities have no attraction to the average buyer. It is too ugly and too noisy. Such a car can, if at all, only be popular for two to three years at most.' The Beetle went on to be the most successful production car of all time. But then the Beetle was designed by Dr Ferry Porsche, a fact which alone should have made our industry sit up and take notice.

*The British industry's need to make bold statements after the War manifested itself in some worrying forms. This is the frightening 1950 Triumph Mayflower, allegedly considered attractive at the time!*

While the Morris promised to be the car everyone hoped to own, the beautiful Jaguar was a symbol of a new brazen flair in car styling where the freedom of the road and personal style seemed more important than any restrictive practicality.

The export drive manifested itself in many ways at the Motor Show. Fundamentally, and as the motoring press pointed out, the Show displayed cars principally for the benefit of foreign buyers. Very few of the models on offer could realistically be bought on the domestic market. Secondly, the styling of the cars reflected the markets to which they were designed to appeal. American styling influences were strong across the board. The new Vauxhalls and Hillmans, the aforementioned Jowett Javelin and the Standard Vanguard all flaunted a Stateside image. Only the sports car remained quintessentially British, or at least European, a 'look' which Americans were prepared to pay a high price for.

Perhaps the most beneficial pay-off from the export business was a far greater maturity in the design and reliability of British cars. They had to be more rugged to survive many foreign operational conditions. Suspension and steering systems had to be more sophisticated, heating and ventilation systems had not only to exist but also to work properly (although few did),

and engines had to be more powerful and reliable. Thankfully, the ill-conceived 'horse-power tax' which had plagued the British motor industry since 1920 was lifted in 1945, allowing engine designers to abandon their previous restrictions. For some extraordinary reason the horse-power rating had been assessed not according to engine displacement, but according to engine bore size. A high displacement engine – so essential for achieving power – therefore had to be obtained by lengthening the piston stroke rather than by increasing the bore diameter. The result was engines which were neither efficient nor inherently smooth. With the tax abandoned several classic engine designs therefore appeared at the 1948 Motor Show, not least in the Morris Minor and the Jaguar XK120, the engines for which both remained in production in one form or another for decades to come.

It took two more years for Britain to throw off its austere lifestyle and return to something akin to motoring normality. By then rationing of all kinds had gone (even if petrol tax was doubled in 1950) and most car manufacturers had displayed their new state-of-the-art models at the Motor Show. In the words of Peter Falconer: 'It was a wonderful feeling to see motoring coming back – the sheer enjoyment of being able to buy a new car and being able to choose it. It took until the 1950s to achieve that, but it meant so much.'

*Fortunately, William Lyons's 1949 Jaguar XK120 was such a superbly styled and capable car that such traumatised misdemeanours as the Mayflower were conveniently forgotten. Here Mrs L. Snow shows off her rare right-hand drive example at the Eastbourne Concours in 1952.*

*Chapter 5*

# ROAD HOGS

*I*n 1966 Hugh Tracey published the motoring diary of his father, who was Devon's first motorised country doctor. Doctors were among the first to recognise the use of the motor car for professional purposes and Hugh Tracey's father became something of an enthusiast, despite his near daily trials and tribulations. He wrote to Hugh's mother on 21st September 1907 about the new 10/12 Peugeot he had bought – his first car:

*My own darling,*

*I am just wild with delight. This car is an event in our lives and I am sure we will enjoy it amazingly. Brane, the chauffeur, is a perfect driver, and can let her all out... He has definitely used only one of the brakes once this whole day. The other he has not touched. If you use the brakes a lot it is bad driving, strains the engine to pieces and wears the tyres out in no time.*

Later diary entries are more telling:

*October 5: Ran over and damaged S.H. Thomas' dog. Its own fault entirely owing to almost complete deafness.*
*October 25: Met a herd of cows three miles the other side of Totnes. Bent axle, steering rod, lamp brackets... after striking two or three cows.*

The bad driver was born on the first day that man drove the motor car: bad either through his or her lack of mechanical understanding or sympathy; or bad because of the manner in which the car was driven with regard to other road users. The Hon C.S. Rolls could be cited as England's first celebrated bad driver when he terrified the commoners between Cambridge and Monmouth on his epic winter drive home in his nearly new 1896 Peugeot. But the anti-social nature of Rolls's escapades (see Chapter One) were far more the norm than unique. For the first 15 or so years of motoring in Britain cars were driven almost exclusively for recreational purposes and only by the very wealthy. As discussed before, country doctors aside, such motorists were usually arrogant, extremely selfish and brazenly upper-class. Sitting aloft in their tall and wonderful mechanical monsters, passengers clad in offensive fashions, the early motorists would look down on everyone nearby, before dowsing them in a cloud of filthy road-dust – a lasting memento of the rich kid's fleeting, noisy visit.

Nowadays, bad driving and even road-rage are largely the product of crowded roads and cocooned drivers who feel protected in their cars from the abuse of others around them. But in the early days bad

*Pages 138-139: A 24hp Napier has met its end over the cliff at Bexhill-on-Sea in 1907. Clearly the most exciting thing to happen there for some considerable time...*

*Below: 'Sound yer 'orn!' 'Sound your aitches!' Motoring did plenty to perpetuate the gulf between the social classes in Britain.*

driving was brought about by poor (or non-existent) driver instruction, lack of mechanical sympathy, no highway codes, unsafe automobiles driving too quickly on poor road surfaces, and 'scorching'.

'Scorching' was a term coined in the Edwardian era for motorists who drove too fast. At a time when the national speed limit was set at 20mph (as it was from 1903 until 1st January 1931, after which it was abolished on the open road thanks to the New Road Traffic Act), 'scorching' was easy to do, but unlike today when a speeder may be a member of any social class driving any modern car, in those days the 'scorcher' was bound to be either a headstrong chauffeur misbehaving in one of his master's motors, or the master himself behaving like a playboy. And there were no greater playboys in the Edwardian and Vintage eras than the rich undergraduates of Cambridge University. Although hardly representative of the experience of the average British motorist, the high-speed capers of the Varsity 'scorchers' in the most powerful cars of the day summed up every heartfelt gripe of the anti-motoring lobby, and it's not hard to see why. C.S. Rolls might have been the first of the Cambridge 'scorchers', but others of his generation built far more dare-devil reputations.

Kenelm 'Bill' Lee Guinness, who later (in 1922) broke the land speed record at 134mph at Brooklands driving the 350hp V12 Sunbeam, owned a

*This is an accident in Guildford in 1907, and one can't help feeling that the motorist was speeding, given the limit in force...*

fearsome 40hp racing Panhard while he was at Cambridge, a similar car to the type that won the Circuit du Nord in 1902. Guinness's parents lived in Windsor, and Bill delighted in wheel-spinning the racer up the wet cobblestones of Windsor High Street while the engine raced on a high throttle. The fearful noise and attitude of the car were hated by the local police. Bill and his brother, Sir Algernon 'Algy' Guinness, had a sensational collection of fast cars, including the ultimate production sports car of the era, the Mercedes 60, and many monstrous Darracqs, including the famous 100hp car that broke the land speed record at 104mph in 1904 (driven by Baras) and the fabled 200hp V8 which broke the record again in 1905 at 109mph (driven by Hémery).

The 200 Darracq was bought by Algy in London – 'The inferno of noise, flame, smoke and fumes from the short open exhaust pipes... impressed Algy considerably', wrote G.R.N. Minchin in his splendid book of motoring memories *Under My Bonnet*. The car was towed to the family workshops in Datchet behind Lord Anneley's 1903 Mercedes 'at about 40 all the way'! From there its illustrious career as Algy's road-and-record car began. At one point in 1908 he topped 120mph in the 200 on Saltburn Sands. The use of such a car on the road today is beyond imagination. A fellow Cambridge student, H.W. Bunbury, wrote: 'I have ridden in the mechanic's seat in very many racing cars between the years 1903 and 1939, but for a real thrill and for pure joy, nothing ever came up to a full-throttle run on the 200, with the car in Algy Guinness's capable hands.'

### BACKWARDS RACING IN CAMBRIDGE

Road racing seemed all but the norm for the decadent Cambridge students. Minchin recalls that racing in reverse down the winding Jesus Lane was a particular favourite. On one occasion a Chenard-Walcker and an Isotta Fraschini got locked together, side by side, before crashing at full speed through the doorway of a house...

One Sunday morning Messrs Van Raalte and Rhodes-Moorhouse challenged each other to a race through Cambridge, 'from Market Square to the station,' recalled Minchin, 'about 1 1/4 to 1 1/2 miles, the loser to pay all the fines.' That they were reasonably sure to be caught and fined was indication enough that the wealthy young men had little regard for the law. For this Sunday's competition Van Raalte was driving a 140hp Minerva 'Kaiserpreis' and Rhodes-Moorhouse a 90hp chain-drive Grand Prix Fiat – the Formula One racing cars of their generation (only far more dangerous). Minchin recalled: 'Sir George Clark, his brother "Tubby" and I kept the crossroads clear on the long straight

---

### DOING THE TON IN TOWN

By its nature a sports car is designed to break the law because, to enjoy its potential, speed limits have to be broken. The Piccadilly-based Hundred Mile an Hour Club was formed with precisely that in mind: you qualified only if you had driven on Park Lane at 100mph, witnessed by a club official. 'Proper chap' racing drivers like Archie Scott Brown and Tony Rolt apparently achieved the magic 'ton' in the early hours of the morning. 'I remember one rather marvellous night', tells Red Daniells, 'when we were leaving a little café in Chelsea and we all descended onto the Embankment and roared along both sides of the road – seven or eight vintage motors. Suddenly a young policeman stepped out to stop us. Some of us went on the pavement to avoid him, others went up Sloane Street, some went over the bridge and down the pie-stall straight and some went straight on. With us all disseminated all he could do was shout after us.'

Left: Malcolm Campbell
makes the fastest ascent
of the day at the Essex
County and Southend
Automobile Club's
Thundersley hill climb
in 1921 aboard his
1912 GP Peugeot.
Such exotic performance
cars were driven on the
road by wealthy
young 'scorchers'.

Below: Algy Guinness
exceeds 120mph at
Saltburn Sands in
1908 on the mighty
Darracq 200.

rené ponsot

stretch by the Roman Catholic Cathedral, and they passed us at about 85mph.' Van Raalte won quite easily, and the £40 of court fines were paid by Rhodes-Moorhouse, who, incidentally, was told by the Chairman of the Bench 'what a worthless and good-for-nothing young man' he was. Five years later First Airman Rhodes-Moorhouse died in the First World War during a feat of exceptional bravery. He was awarded the Victoria Cross.

Minchin wrote that he doubted that any motorist had ever been summoned as often as a fellow Cambridge student, E.H. Lees. Lees owned a bright red 27/80 'Prince Henry' Métallurgique two-seater – another huge racing car built for the German Prince Henry tour (in reality a road race) in 1909. Lees had persuaded Eric Dickson, a chum of his at Cambridge, to time him over a fast stretch of road from Newmarket to Thetford, but when Dickson sat ready with his stopwatch, a broadly smiling policeman joined him, knowing what was afoot. Dickson recalled: 'I heard the car a mile or two away coming all-out towards the piece of road we had measured... but when Lees appeared the policeman's jaw dropped, his eyes boggled and I heard him mutter "my Gawd". Although he had started his watch, he fortunately had forgotten to stop it! I made it 92 mph.'

On another occasion Lees accelerated through Newmarket in the 'Met' with a deliberately wide-open throttle and scared a group of horses being led to graze over the other side of the road. As the terrified horses bolted away and out of sight Lees began to realise the seriousness of his crime, committed as it was in Newmarket of all places – the traditional and hallowed home of English racehorses. He drove on to London and dumped his car at the garage of a fellow University friend, Cecil Chandler, where he changed its colour from red to green overnight and swapped its number plates with those of Chandler's magnificent Renault limousine (another remarkable student motor). The ruse worked and Lees escaped the police again.

*Left: Road racing was common in Italy where race craft could be learnt at the expense of the public's safety, but such romantic foolhardiness was never tolerated in Britain.*

*Below: Edwardian cars carrying luxurious coachwork were seldom strong and were usually overweight. Spectacular-looking accidents could occur even at quite modest collision speeds.*

*Above: One of the British Isles' only true road races was the Gordon Bennett cup held in Ireland. Gabriel in his Mors arrives on the Dublin dockside in 1903.*

*Right: A Model T Ford misses the bridge on Barnes Common after an incident in 1914.*

Minchin also owned one of the Prince Henry 'Mets' (apparently only three were built) and even ran Malcolm Campbell's first 'Bluebird' Darracq as a road car for some years, until 1920, but he is principally remembered for his love of 40/50 Rolls-Royce Ghosts. It was while Minchin was riding in the back of a London-Edinburgh type Ghost in France that he and Lees nearly met their end. It was 1913 and Minchin and his party were making their way to the French Grand Prix at Amiens. They were on a long straight piece of road, cruising at a steady 70mph in the Rolls, when Minchin 'chanced to glance to my left. There through the trees I saw a flash of red moving at right-angles towards us. A road lay in front, crossing our path, but providentially our driver ignored it. Nor had he seen the red streak moving at over 90mph towards us, or he would surely have momentarily lifted his foot. As it was, we were a few feet in front, but as the other car shot across behind us, I could have leaned over and touched it! It was Lees... in his Métallurgique, once again a bright red two-seater...'

One has to remember that at the time of such rich-kid 'scorching' the sports car had yet to be invented, and the Varsity road hogs were little more than the hot-rodders of their day. The likes of Lees and Guinness had little choice but to buy a secondhand racing car or, better yet, a used land-speed-record car. Although British six-cylinder cars became fashionable between 1905 and 1909, these engines were designed to be smooth and quiet, rather than revvable and sporting, and next to the established Mercedes 40 or 60 or Panhard 50, the Best of British just wouldn't cut the mustard. With British sixes out of the question (the super-rare and expensive Ariel Simplex excluded), the only other route for the scorchers was to strip down a six-cylinder Fiat, Bianchi, Itala, Mors or CGV, if you could find one. The trouble was that such exotics were very rare and wickedly expensive; far better to buy a used 'Merc' or a redundant racing car to outrun the constables.

By the beginning of the First World War the venerable six-cylinder engine was positively overshadowed, not only by the usual foreign big bangers but also by the arrival of several more technically refined devices – cars that announced the coming of the Vintage era. In the words of Michael Sedgwick writing in *The Autocar*: 'The brute-force school – lots of litres plus chain drive – persisted in Germany and Italy up to the War... ; but representative of a new generation were Pomeroy's Vauxhall, Birkigt's Hispano-Suiza, Porsche's Austro-Daimler and the first Bugattis... There was

*Two pictures showing a handsome but embarrassed Rolls-Royce Phantom needing classical assistance while touring Norway. What excitement for the locals, as presumably Rolls-Royces weren't often seen in those parts.*

*The damage is substantial but the Morris (top) and Austin merely gave each other a glancing high-street blow. Note the Austin's broken windscreen. Triplex safety glass was made in England from 1911, but there is no evidence of it here.*

even a brief sports car vogue in America, which bred some splendid devices, notably the Mercer 35.'

The beginning of the Vintage era in 1919 marked the birth of the sports car, and with it came a whole new incentive to drive badly. But while the wealthy could indulge in madcap motoring with unrivalled gay abandon, the attraction of messing about in motors was universal. With the space to enjoy tomfoolery without too much chance of either being caught or causing too much danger to others, most young men behind the wheel were apt to take advantage of the vehicle's technological shortcomings in the search for a thrill.

Pre-war van driver Fred Blackman admits to numerous 'bad driving' excesses in his youth, which had been spent in London. Before the introduction of the driving test in 1935, getting a driving licence was a simple question of applying for one. Fred did this as soon as he was 16. With vans and lorries often speed-regulated to between 20 and 30mph, the potential for driving like a hooligan was limited to cornering and braking manoeuvres. The road surfaces, made of 'quiet' tar-covered wooden blocks in London, became extremely slippery after rainfall, especially if the tar had worn off and a slurry of horse manure had settled on the glass-like finishes. 'You see, with the back wheels you've got one set of linings for your hand-brake and another set of linings for your foot-brake, so if you want a spectacular skid (these kids have got nothing on it now) you put the handbrake on and slam the footbrake on and so you go round. I went round three times on Hendon Broadway once and straightened up and carried on...' On another occasion Fred was less lucky and hit some tramlines as he spun round. 'I tipped the bloody vehicle over, and the copper could see that it was my fault and he was going to pinch me, but I think they got talked out of it by my governor.'

Negotiating with the police was an important part of intelligent road behaviour, especially if you were a regular motoring offender. On the one hand police, even in Greater London, got to know a local driver and his vehicle, so it was as well to get on with the police rather than gain a reputation for being troublesome. On the other hand, in those days before fixed penalty fines, most summons and police judgements were subject to negotiation. In the words of Fred Blackman: 'When the copper pulls you up you've got to start talking and talking nice... because as soon as you start hollering and swearing, out comes the book and you're done.'

Arthur Jeddere-Fisher, stalwart member of England's Vintage Sports Car Club, long-time Vintage car motorist and a senior member of the judiciary, recalls similar importance in behaving civilly towards the police, immediately after the Second World War. 'I used to get stopped quite frequently by the police but they were always fairly decent about it. Many of them were motoring enthusiasts themselves, of course, and you could usually talk your speeding offence down from 60 to 45 with a bit of chatter.'

Arthur was at university after the war and, at a time when you could buy quite a serious Vintage sports car – like a Vauxhall 30/98 – for £10 to 15, he and his mates drove some fairly spectacular machinery. 'There was an awful lot of racing on the road at that time. We probably drove too fast, but the war was over and having got through that we weren't frightened of much.'

## MOTOR CHALLENGES

Road racing, either amateur or professional (in so far as racing was a profession), existed right from the dawn of motoring, especially in France where the relatively good main roads witnessed frequent international challenges. In fact, the first official land speed record was set in 1898 on the Achères road, near Paris, on 18th December. Count Gaston de Chasseloup-Laubat achieved a flying time of 39.3mph on his Jeantaud electric car. While the Count's speed might not have seemed dangerously excessive, the record was nearly doubled on the same stretch of road at 65.8mph only the following year. Furthermore, the tradition of land speed record-breaking on public roads continued in France until June 1924. That month alone, the record was broken twice, once by René Thomas in the V12, 10.6-litre Delage at 143.3mph and six days later by Ernest Eldridge in the monstrous 21.7-litre Fiat Mephistopheles at 146mph, both cars on the road in Arpajon.

In Britain, racing on unclosed public roads has never been allowed, and our sportsmen would generally travel to other countries in Europe to compete in them. Classic events such as the Mille Miglia in Italy, the Targa Florio in Sicily and the Carrera Panamericana during the 1950s in Mexico often took a tremendous toll of human life between them (driver and spectator).

*The expression on the face of the front-seat passenger of this speeding Vauxhall 30/98 sums up the thrill of driving fast. The driver's reversed cap was crucial if it was to stay on at speed. The style became a hallmark of the 'scorcher'.*

*The frequent price of road racing – a Baroness has crashed her Cisitalia on the 1953 Targa Florio in Sicily. Accidents such as these put an eventual end to many a foreign road race.*

The French had started the road-racing tradition before the turn of the century with races from Paris to Bordeaux, Marseilles, and later Berlin and Vienna, among other places. But even after the terrible Paris–Madrid race in 1903, which was stopped in Bordeaux after 34 competitors were killed (including Marcel Renault), mostly in unrelated accidents, road racing continued in France and Italy. It still exists today, albeit unofficially, as part of retrospective events like the Tour de France and Mille Miglia, run for the benefit of historic sports and racing cars.

It didn't seem fair. With many Italian and French racing drivers able to practise their racing every weekend on the public roads (to say nothing of the likes of the great Fangio, who learnt his unrivalled craft on the roads in Argentina), and with road races allowed in America until 1924 (even if the banked board circuits gained popularity from around 1916), the budding British racing driver felt underprivileged. He had to rely on the few circuit races that existed in this country and the odd weekend hill climb meeting. Brooklands in Surrey, Britain's first purpose-built race track, was crucially opened in 1907, Donington in Leicestershire followed much later in 1933, and London's Crystal Palace circuit didn't open until 1937. All Britain's other great circuits, notably Goodwood and Silverstone (such as it was), came after the Second World War. For road racing – where the racing craft was perfected – only Ireland and the Isle of Man ever obliged, Ireland in 1903 with the Gordon Bennett trial, and much later from 1928 at the Ards/Dundrod circuit near Belfast. From 1922 the Tourist Trophy race was staged on the Isle of Man, but such places were far-flung and hardly facilitated regular racing practice. The result was inevitable law-breaking as the relatively empty English roads played host to illegal challenges between young men driving everything from speed-regulated delivery vans to out-and-out Grand Prix cars.

Of course, the average family car was not fast in the 1920s or even the 1930s. As late as 1935 the fastest car road-tested by *The Motor* magazine that year was a Railton at 107mph. Classic British 'bull-dog' sports cars like the Le Mans-winning Blower Bentley or the 4.5-litre Lagonda were not 100mph cars, contrary to what one might imagine. In fact the popular 100mph sports car couldn't be bought in Britain until the early 1950s, when cars like the Jaguar XK120, Austin Healey 100/4 and Triumph TR2 finally became available.

## THE COURTESY COPS

Rising accident rates in the late 1930s gave rise to the Police Accident Prevention Unit and the Courtesy Cops. Courtesy Cops were first-class police drivers who placed themselves by busy roads as a deterrent to potential offenders. Spying a Courtesy Cop didn't mean you were about to be 'nicked', but it might have reminded the offending motorist that he was breaking the law. Such a passive form of public policing might seem extraordinary today, but the Courtesy Cops were respected and effective. Only the Second World War put a stop to them. 'I think it's a great pity we haven't still got Courtesy Cops,' says Elwyn Reed. 'They knew their job... and if they saw anyone doing anything wrong they would simply pull alongside and tell them. And that way people learnt. They were never juniors, always mature people and they had the right temperament.'

'At any time before the Second World War, most cars would have been hard pushed to reach 75mph (the fast V8 Ford would only make 66mph, the racy Lagonda 2-litre topped only 70mph, and the supercharged version only 88mph),' explains the motoring journalist Ronald Barker. In the 1920s there were still a lot of Edwardian cars on the road, and 35-40mph cruising was considered ambitious by most, even in the newest devices available.

D.B. 'Bunny' Tubbs wrote in *Autocar*: 'Straights were so rare that some drivers could really only 'let her out' only once or twice a year, in places like Hartford Bridge Flats, the Great North Road, East Anglia, Salisbury Plain or the Hog's Back.' Bunny continued: 'Then – as now – there were few places you could use the performance of a fast car... On the average cross-country journey the non-sporting driver of, say, an 11.9hp AC, was pleased if he could average a mile every two minutes – 30mph.' And, as Ronald Barker explains: 'It wasn't speed that was at the heart of bad driving, it was the lack of control,' which in the early days was due to driver ineptitude, poor grip, variable road surfaces and brakes operating only the rear wheels

*The greatest road race of them all was the Mille Miglia in Italy. Here the Argentine ace Fangio crosses the line to take second position in 1955. The race was won by the 25-year-old Englishman Stirling Moss driving a similar Mercedes car. Moss drove for ten hours and seven minutes to cover the 990-mile route (all on public roads) at an average speed of 97.9mph.*

## ELWYN REED REMEMBERS – BECOMING A DRIVING INSTRUCTOR

*Having served in the ambulance service during the war, and having loved cars ever since her boyfriend's father allowed her to drive his in 1933, Elwyn decided to become a driving instructor and enrolled in the Kent School of Motoring. She became Britain's first woman driving instructor and the first woman to run her own driving school.*

*'The number of accidents that went on in the thirties was higher than it is today. It wasn't only the car driver that was to blame. It was the cyclist and the pedestrian as well – none of them seemed to be aware of anything. There were no pedestrian crossings, so people used to dart across whenever they felt like it. Children on bicycles were all over the place. There were extremely bad drivers with the wrong temperament: "I can do this and I can do that and blow everybody else." Such people used to say the best way to go down the road in the fog – there was terrible fog – even if it was the main road, was to drive slap down the middle of it... And the roads weren't swept like they should have been – there was rubble and bricks and stones and wood and so on. And the trees weren't kept trim so that they would clear the road. And we didn't have road signs, or white lines down the middle of roads. These were the causes of the enormous numbers of accidents.*

*'The key to good driving is, firstly, to love it and enjoy it and, secondly, to love your motor car and enjoy that. Then you must try and understand people as best you can; practise everything that you know is right, and never stop concentrating. It's difficult to do that, especially when you have a car full of people, but it's absolutely essential. I had one lady student in her mid-sixties who was a real scatterbrain. We'd be driving along the road and she would say: "Ooo! Look! I know that lady, she's got new curtains..." She passed her test at the 17th attempt after 450 driving lessons.'*

(four-wheel brakes were still unusual in the 1930s except on later new cars). 'The road surfaces were horribly inconsistent,' remembers Ronald, 'and there was little more alarming to the driver than a change from tarmac to gravel or shingle, especially at night when you really couldn't see it coming.'

### AN ALARMING RATE OF ACCIDENTS

According to policeman Ted Teer: 'There is a great difference in being in a hurry and going fast. Too many people take chances; too many people are impatient – impatience is the problem.' Ted was one of the very first instructors at Hendon Police College. In fact, the Police Flying Squad was instigated in the early 1920s using police cars fitted with two-way radios, but during the 1930s the road-accident rate was alarmingly high, and police mobile duties were greatly expanded, drivers often graduating through the Hendon school.

At the beginning of the thirties there were 7305 road deaths in Britain and a little over one million cars in use. The government responded with the New Traffic Act which, apart from curiously dispensing with the speed limit for four years (it was reintroduced at 30mph in towns in 1935), also brought about the introduction of the driving test in 1935 and various traffic safety measures, including the 'Belisha' beacon in 1934 (named after the Minister of Transport, Leslie Hore-Belisha). Although the peacetime road death-rate total continued to rise, peaking in 1939 at 8272, by then there were twice as many cars on Britain's roads.

Perhaps the most significant step in reducing bad driving and cutting the number of accidents was the introduction in 1967 of the breathalyser test for the detection of drunk drivers. Incredibly, no specific drink-drive legislation existed before this date, a policeman having no greater powers to stop a motorist for drink-driving than he had to stop a pedestrian for being drunk and disorderly. And even if a motorist were stopped, the most sophisticated test measures the police employed were to smell the driver's breath or to walk the accused down a white line (presumably not the terribly convenient one in the centre of the road). As Fred Blackman recalls: 'Drinking and driving? They're on about it today, but we never bothered. We used to always finish up at the Bull and Bush in Hampstead. There was a side road there – you'd see all the laundry vans parked round the corner. We were in there – Shove Ha'penny, a few pints – and away we'd go. Once I said to the missus after I'd gone to bed: "I've gotta go... I can't remember putting the van away..."'

The year 1967 was highly significant in Britain's road safety history for several other reasons, too: seat belts were made compulsory in new cars,

*Lancashire policewomen stand by their newly-delivered 1957 MG As which were to be their new patrol cars. The police often drove exciting sports cars while on patrol, ranging from Sunbeam Tigers to Daimler SP250s.*

*The coming of the electric traffic light did much to reduce congestion and road accidents. The first in Britain were fitted in the village of Cottingham near Hull in 1931.*

the 70mph speed limit was introduced on derestricted roads, and the annual MoT test had to be taken by all cars more than three years old, whereas the previous MoT (introduced in 1961) had applied to cars that were more than ten years old.

With so many improvements made to road safety legislation in 1967, to say nothing of the huge advances made in car design since, and the introduction of the compulsory wearing of front seatbelts in Britain in 1983, the specific effects of the breathalyser test on reducing road deaths is difficult to quantify. However, today there are ten times as many cars on the roads as there were in 1930, and twice as many as there were in 1967, yet road deaths are almost half as numerous as was the case throughout the sixties. Although in America twice as many citizens as died during the wars have been killed by car accidents, and although those travelling by car are still around a hundred times more likely to die than those who travel by air, we should remain content that, road-rage or not, we are much safer driving today than we ever have been before.

## CULTIVATING A SENSE OF PROPORTION

*Road-rage is nothing new, as the satirists Fougasse and McCullough noted in this stream-of-consciousness parody as early as 1935:*

*'Of course most of the trouble on the road would be avoided if people would only cultivate a sense of proportion and stop driving much too fast in the hope of saving five minutes... and then they would be able to drive a perfectly beautiful machine along a perfectly wonderful road in perfect peace and toleration as I'm doing now instead of thinking they've got to roar about and hoot and risk everyone's lives by cutting in like that fellow in the blue car in front which only makes them get into a filthy state of nerves... and if half-baked louts like this man just in front didn't glue themselves to the crown of the road and make one hoot at them till one's completely deaf and if half-witted pedestrians like that one didn't simply hurl themselves under the wheels whenever one appeared suddenly round a bend, and if this type of lorry-driving fiend didn't lumber about the roads hiding everything in front so that one has just got to trust blindly to luck every time one cuts in front of them on a corner and if absolute raving lunatics like this one didn't hurtle at full speed along a main road quite oblivious of the fact that we might be dashing suddenly out of a side road... and if everything else on the road didn't take a perfectly hellish delight in getting in one's way and making one lose precious minutes and... Blast you! Will you get out of my... CRASH!'*

*Above: The breathalyser test was introduced in 1967, before which no legislation or widely accepted means of testing consumption existed. Road-death statistics fell dramatically after its introduction.*

*Left: An early police radar in operation, as propped on the boot of a police MG A.*

# EPILOGUE

*I*t happens every morning at about 8 o'clock. There I am, letting my breakfast settle while listening to Radio 3, when suddenly there's a raucous fanfare of horns and a percussion of discordant expletives. No, I don't refer to a sudden invasion of contemporary jazz, but to the appalling orchestrations of that modern operatic ritual, the clash of the motorists – a pair of raging drivers abusing each other in the rush-hour traffic outside my window. All those flared nostrils, gnashing teeth, salivations and gesticulations are enough to upset anybody's day before it's begun, especially if not 50 yards from your own front room.

Occasionally, if the vocabulary and volume are monumental enough, I peer down at the mini-roundabout in fascination to see what could possibly be the cause of such aggression. There hasn't been a road death or an injury; there hasn't been a car-jacking or a smash-and-grab; there hasn't even been an incident in which someone's precious car has been threatened, much less grazed. Oh, no. Such street-fighting is born out of a misunderstanding of the rules of the road, or more usually, a little driving ineptitude by one which is not appreciated by the other.

But this is the 1990s, and with the decade came a whole new vocabulary in the dictionary of motor mania. From road-rage to car-jacking, gridlock to exhaust-induced asthma, motoring today is a far cry from the freedom ideal it represented even as recently as 30 years ago.

In the news today as I write, *Autocar*, the longest-established motoring magazine in the world (100 years old in November 1995), leads its news pages with the words: 'Motorists face five months of traffic jam misery as the three crucial arteries feeding west London are hit by roadworks. Up to 300,000 drivers a day are being caught' – costing, incidentally, 13,500 man hours per 10-mile stretch of tailback. Furthermore, the Chancellor's new budget, announced yesterday as I write, has effectively slashed Britain's road-building programme. Reporting as much, *The Independent* newspaper quoted a road-building lobbyist as describing the action as 'the worst day for Britain's infrastructure since the Romans left'. The same newspaper, six pages on, reports that the Inter-Governmental Panel on Climate Change (IPCC) has announced that the governments of more than 90 nations have finally agreed that the billions of tons of carbon dioxide and other 'greenhouse gases' spewed into the earth's atmosphere from the burning of, among

*The quintessential pre-Second World War motoring ideal: a superb SS1 Tourer receives a welcome salute from an AA patrolman. Never did England make a more beautiful and able sports tourer, and never was motoring more pleasurable.*

other things, fossil fuels in cars, is having a 'discernible... influence on global climate'. At current rates of pollution the world's average temperature will have risen, says the report, by a 'hugely damaging 3.5°C' in a century's time. Such is the topicality of motoring's problems.

As the morning rush-hour subsides, so too do the motorists' tempers, and my day away from the road-rage outside commences, only the occasional 'parp' of an irritated horn denoting a road too busy by half, or the wail of an errant car alarm signifying that an intruding housefly has been caught by the in-car infra-red.

In the evening tired commuters seldom have the energy to summon up the venomous blood to rage. Instead, the mature and weary snake and sneer their way home to rejuvenate in time for tomorrow's battles, while the young and obnoxious focus their testosterone into high-volume escapism behind the wheels of Teutonic coupés and hot hatchbacks they can ill afford to buy, let alone maintain. The last hoorah of the young man's motoring dream?

And it doesn't matter whether it's the kid with the Gti cruising to be cool, or the middle-class mum in her new four-wheel drive taking the children to school; they all choose to drive, to a greater or lesser extent, for the same reasons: they need to get around as conveniently and quickly as possible; they want to project their status and identity; and they want to experience all that is bound up in that 100-year-old adage 'the freedom of the road'.

As long as motoring represents personal freedom and identity, and as long as you are what you drive and you enjoy the sense of freedom and the real practicalities of freedom that driving provides, then motor mania is inevitable – irrespective of the influences of fossil fuels and greenhouse gases, gridlocks and road-rage, traffic wardens and wheel clamps.

Fortunately, technological advances have been so great during very recent years that ZEVs (zero emission vehicles), not least electrically powered cars, are now real possibilities for the future, at least in limited markets. But quite how the larger-scale and growing problems of traffic density, pollution and limited raw material supply can be solved remains wholly unfathomable, at least to conventional scientists.

In the short term, car-makers with no practical fuel alternatives available concentrate their inventive resources on making their fossil-fuelled inventions more efficient. Ultimately, if they are still unable to provide the miraculous solutions that are required, they know that it will be the governments which will put a stop to motoring and motor mania. Always assuming that the planet doesn't do so first.

*The inevitable post-Second World War motoring nightmare. Endless roadbuilding is required to cope with the ever-increasing number of motorists in Britain. Despite the environmental implications and government budget cutbacks, more roads will still be required to defeat the gridlock problem.*

**FURTHER READING**

The following publications have provided valuable research material while compiling *Motor Mania*:

*A-Z of Cars, 1945-1970*, by Michael Sedgwick and Mark Gillies (Temple Press, 1986)

*Austerity Motoring*, by Andrew Lane (Shire Publications, 1987)

*Automania*, by Julian Pettifer and Nigel Turner (Collins, 1984)

*The Automobile – The First Century*, by David Burgess Wise, William Boddy and Brian Laban (Orbis Publishing, 1983)

*The Centenary of the Car*, by Andrew Whyte (Octopus, 1984)

*The Complete Encyclopedia of Motorcars*, edited by G.N. Georgano (Ebury Press, 1968)

*The Country Garage*, by Llyn E. Morris (Shire Publications, 1985)

*Father's First Car*, by Hugh Tracey (Routledge & Kegan Paul, 1966)

*Flywheel: Memories of the Open Road*, by Tom Swallow, Arthur H. Pill and the members of the Muhlberg Motor Club, Stalag IVB, Germany 1944-1945 (Webb and Bower, 1987)

*Great Moments in Motoring*, by Phil Drackett (Phoenix House, 1958)

*The Kings of the Road*, by Ken W. Purdy (Arrow Books, 1955)

*Motorcade*, by Maurice A. Hammond (G. Bell and Sons, 1969)

*Motoring and the Mighty*, by Richard Garrett (Stanley Paul, 1971)

*Motoring in the Thirties*, by Graham Robson (PSL, 1979)

*Motoring Milestones*, by contributors to *Autocar* magazine (IPC Transport Press Ltd, 1979)

*One Hundred Motoring Years*, by contributors to *Autocar* magazine (IPC Business Press Ltd, 1973)

*One Hundred Years of Motoring*, by Raymond Flower and Michael Wynn Jones (McGraw-Hill and the RAC, 1981)

*One Hundred Years of the Motor Car*, by various contributors (Book Club Associates by arrangement with Arnoldo Mondadori S.p.A. and William Collins Sons and Co Ltd, 1985)

*Recreation – Motoring*, by John Marshall (Hodder and Stoughton, 1954)

*Seeing Britain from an Austin*, by Alison D. Murray (Ed J. Burrow and Co)

*The Story of Veteran and Vintage Cars*, by Cyril Posthumus (Hamlyn, 1977)

*Under My Bonnet*, by G.R.N. Minchin (Motoraces Book Club, 1967)

*Veteran and Vintage Cars*, by Peter Roberts (Octopus Books, 1974)

*Veteran Motor Cars*, by Michael Ware (Shire Publications, 1983)

## ACKNOWLEDGEMENTS

The author and publishers are grateful to the following individuals and organisations for their help in the research and compilation of *Motor Mania*:

Brian Asquith; Harry Baggs; G.L. Barron; Fred Blackman; Tim Clarke; Red Daniells; Gilbert Everett; Peter Falconer; David Guest; Dick Hardy; Arthur Jeddere-Fisher; Niel F. Fraser (sen); James Lazenby; Ralph Lee; George Llewelyn; Rod Mackay; Jim Oliver; Gerald Palmer; Freddie Passey; C.W. Pearsall; Roy Shannon; Ted Teer; Elwyn Reed; William P. Roe; Joan Ruston; Tom Swallow; Elizabeth Vowles; Arthur Walker; Anthony Wood.

Special thanks to Ronald Barker and Mick Walsh, Editor-in-Chief of *Classic and Sportscar* magazine; Jonathon Day at the National Motor Museum Library; the Mercedes-Benz Archives, Michael Passmore at the Automobile Association, Howard Smith at Alfred Dunhill, Miranda Taylor at The Punch Cartoon Library and Toby Wilson at Sotheby's Car Department for their kind help with the loan of photographs; Peter Grimsdale, Commissioning Editor at Channel 4; Martin Stockham at The Archive Programme Unit; James Castle, Taylor Downing, Andrew Johnston, Sue Learoyd, Gerald Lorenz, Brigid O'Connell and Kate Riley at Flashback Television Ltd.

The author's personal thanks to Lil, John, Lois and Sarah, for their crucial assistance.

## ILLUSTRATION CREDITS

The Automobile Association: 18 (below), 30 (both), 68-9, 74-5, 114, 156. The Advertising Archive: 71, 72 (above), 126. Illustrated London News/ Bridgeman Art Library: Front cover, 107. BMIHT/Rover Group: 87 (below), 112, 118, 130. Alfred Dunhill Archives: 48 (both). The Mercedes-Benz Archives: 23. The National Motor Museum, Beaulieu: Back cover, 6, 7, 8, 9 (both), 11, 12 (both), 13, 14-5, 16, 17, 18 (above), 20 (both), 27, 28, 31, 33, 34, 35 (both), 36 (both), 37, 39, 40, 41, 42, 43, 44, 45, 46, 47, 49 (both), 50 (both), 54 (both), 55, 56-7, 58, 59 (both), 60 (both), 62 (above), 63, 64, 65, 66 (both), 67, 70, 72 (below), 75, 77 (both), 78 (both), 81, 82-3, 84, 85, 86, 88 (below), 89 (above), 90, 92 (above), 93, 95, 96 (below), 97, 99 (both), 100, 101, 103, 104 (both), 105, 106 (both), 108 (both), 113 (below), 115 (both), 123, 125 (both), 127, 128, 131, 132, 133, 135, 136, 137, 138-9, 141, 143 (above), 145, 146 (both), 147 (both), 148 (both), 149, 155 (above), 157. Reproduced by permission of Punch: 10, 17, 79, 87 (above), 140. Quadrant Picture Library: 62 (below), 80, 88 (above), 92 (below), 96 (above), 109, 110-1, 113 (above), 116-7, 117, 119, 120-1, 122-3, 129, 143 (below), 150, 151, 153, 154, 155 (below). Sotheby's Car Department: 53 (both), 89 (below), 144.